Social Security, Entitlements, Taxes, Etc.

By

Kenneth Chastain

© 2014

To Jan,
My ever-loving and ever-faithful help meet
Who made all things not only possible,
but also precious
Thanks, Love

Table of Contents

4

Social Security: Why We Would All Be Better Off With A Funded System

Senator Nichols from Oklahoma said on This Week in Washington, February 2, 1999, that Americans making $25,000.00 now pay 43.3% of their income in federal income, social security, and Medicare taxes. State and local taxes are in addition to this. –Surely, over 50%, especially if one attempts to calculate the hidden taxes on everything that we buy. After all, corporations and businesses do not pay taxes. They just add the cost of paid taxes into the price of their product or services. Only individuals pay taxes.

The Camden Chronicle, April 9, 1998

Fool's Day and Tax Day both fall in April. A coincidence? Not when you consider that taxes are now the largest item in the average family's budget, exceeding the cost of food, clothing, housing, and transportation combined. And that's not all. The average taxpayer now works until May 9 to satisfy the appetites of federal, state and local governments. At no point in history has "Tax Freedom Day" occurred so late in the year.

Or how's this? Government now confiscates nearly 40 percent of family income. According to the Heritage Foundation, a Washington-based think tank, medieval serfs had to give only one-third of their output to the lord of the manor—and they were considered slaves.

There are a lot of fools on April 1. But on April 15, Washington plays us all for fools.

The social security dilemma. For every person taking money out of social security, there are presently 3.3 persons putting money in. By the year 2030, this ratio will change dramatically . . . by then, it is estimated that there will be only 2 contributors per recipient. Right now, by the way, someone who retires at age 65 will take about 20 years to recoup the total amount he or she has paid in. For the person

who retires in 2005, it'll take 30 years. In the "good old days" (1980), it took only 4 years. FACTFinder, C/O FACT, 318 Hillsboro Avenue, Edwardsville, Illlinois 62025
WSJ Letters to the Editor March 5, 1999

Amity Shlaes's "Greedy Hand" of government is even greedier than described in her excellent Feb. 25 editorial-page article. Ms. Shlaes points out that today's Social Security and Medicare tax of 7.65% is the highest tax for seven out of 10 households. But that is literally only half the story. A second 7.65% of the taxpayer's earnings is taken by the Greedy Hand from the taxpayer's employer . . . Breaking even on 15.3% for most is a flim-flam promise that would make a three-card-monte artist blush. Fortunately, for our Governing Class and the Great Bureaucracy, this outrageous number—a tax of 15.3% on every working American—is little appreciated by the average taxpayer. James Baar
WSJ Letters to the Editor March 5, 1999

Unfortunately for all of us, the trend is now to make taxes more complicated and much higher. In fact, it was recently reported that due to 1,260 changes enacted by Congress and signed by President Clinton in just the past two years, the tax code now stands at 1.5 million words. And for this tax season, the IRS had to develop 11 new forms and revise 177 others. If you itemize and have a bit of investment income, it's estimated that it will take you 22 hours to complete the forms.

Thomas Jefferson: To preserve our independence, we must not let our rulers load us with public debt. . . We must make our choice between economy and liberty, or profusion and servitude. . . . If we can prevent the government from wasting the labor of the people under the pretense of caring for them, they will be happy.

Introduction

I would like to begin this critique of the Social Security system by highlighting several of the words in the title. The phrase "Social Security" is the cover term that has become associated with the multitude of government programs enacted to provide benefits for American citizens, and non-citizens residing in and out of the United States. Of course, the benefits provided are not "social", and they do not provide "security". However, the term is universally accepted, and the original choice of these two words to describe the system surely was a major factor in promoting the acceptance of the various programs. The word "why" implies that an explanation will be forthcoming, and I do intend to explain my belief that we would all be better off without Social Security. The "we" refers to those of us who live in the United States because voluntarily or involuntarily we are all participants in the system. "Would" is a word often used to describe a condition that is not currently a fact. Neither "are" nor "will" in this context would be appropriate because there is no guarantee that a more sensible and beneficial system will be instituted in the future. The meaning of the complete phrase is that we would all be better off if we were to adopt a fiscally sound funded program to replace the present "pay-as-you-go" system. Of course, "all" means everyone living in the United States because everyone is affected either directly or indirectly by the Social Security system. The definition of "better off" in The American Heritage Dictionary is "in a better or wealthier condition". I am using the phrase to mean "in a better condition" although we would certainly be "wealthier" as well. The word "without" obviously means "in the absence of". If Social Security did not exist, our personal and collective lives would be superior to those we now have.

Who Is The Author?

Who am I? What is there in my background to lead me to reject a system that is so widely accepted and vigorously defended by influential segments of the general public? Why would I want to change programs that so many people believe in so strongly?

I grew up on a red-clay forty-acre hill farm in Southern Indiana. My Mother quit school after the eighth grade. When my Father was sixteen, he left school to work in a local factory, a job that he kept, except for one brief period of less than nine months during World War II, until he retired. Mom and Dad were married in the depths of the Great Depression of the thirties. Mom was a homemaker while I was young. When I left home to attend college, she joined Dad as a laborer in a local cabinet factory. Dad's annual salary never reached the $10,000.00 level; Mom's was much less. They both received Social Security. With the yearly COLAs Dad's monthly check reached $965.00 per month; Mom's was just over $300.00. In addition, Dad received a factory pension of $18.00 a month in return for his life of labor.

Mom and Dad always voted for Democrats. In our house President Franklin Delano Roosevelt (FDR) was as close to deity as a politician can become. I can still hear the oft-repeated phrase, "He did more for the working man than any other President that we have ever had." To his last day Dad maintained, "I would not have been able to survive without Social Security," an opinion surely held by millions of other retired Americans.

My first beliefs with regard to politics and economics were influenced strongly by those of my parents. During my early adult years I always voted democratic. I was greatly impressed by Adlai Stevenson in his campaign for the presidency against Dwight Eisenhower, and Eisenhower's election was a total surprise and complete mystery to me. I simply did not understand how the voters could have chosen Ike over the wonderfully eloquent and logical Stevenson.

Experience, however, is indeed a great teacher, and I gradually became more aware of the gap, often gigantic, between politicians' promises and government benefits. In my own case, for example, I was struck by the huge difference between the benefits that I receive from my private pension and those of Social Security, and by the enormous contrast between the freedom that I have to use the first but not the latter.

Who Are The Readers?

To whom am I writing? The intended readers of this analysis are those who have never questioned the validity of the various Social Security programs. They rarely if ever notice the FDICA tax deducted from their paychecks because the deductions occur regularly and automatically. They look forward to the day when they, too, will retire and receive their Social Security check every month. They are convinced that Social Security is a wonderful program, and they remain ready to vote against any politician who even suggests a critical examination of any of the benefits.

What Are The Purposes?

I have four basic goals in preparing this evaluation of Social Security. My primary purpose is to point out as clearly and concisely as possible that the system is fundamentally flawed and that it is destined to collapse eventually. My secondary purpose is to make present Social Security contributors and future Social Security recipients aware that their future financial payments would be much greater with an alternative savings and investment program. My third purpose is to point out the other negative factors associated with the current Social Security system. My fourth purpose is to convince adherents of Social Security that they should support political action to replace the present system with one that will be better for them, for their children, and for our country economically, socially, and politically.

What Is the Present-Day Situation Regarding Retirement and Retirement Income?

In industrialized societies workers commonly think of retirement as a period of time in later life when they do not have to go to work to earn their living. They leave their job comfortable in the assumption that they will be supported economically during their remaining years without any further labor. They have worked and paid into their Social Security system most of their adult life, and now the time has arrived to sit back and do nothing, if that is their choice. Freed from the necessity of supporting themselves and their family, they may play checkers, work around the house, or go fishing, but they do not have to keep a job. They do not have to work to live. They have reached that "golden" period of life when they can devote themselves to complete independence of activity.

However, the concept of reaching an age at which one does not work, or have to work, is relatively recent. During most of the history of our country, as well as that of other countries, people did not retire. They kept working as long as they were physically able to do so. They were a respected and valuable part of a nuclear family unit. There was work to be done, and they contributed to the daily routine of raising food, taking care of animals, maintaining the buildings, cooking, cleaning the house, and caring for children. They were experienced, and their advice was sought. They belonged, and they played a vital role in the family unit and in their local society. They continued to make needed contributions. There was no thought of simply dropping out and doing what one wanted, first because that would not have been proper while everyone else was doing something needed and second because it was not economically possible. When one was physically unable to work, there was no problem. Family members took care of their own kin.

Two changes occurred that fundamentally altered the productive and useful role of the elderly in society. The first was the industrialization of the country. Entrepreneurs like Henry Ford built huge factories to mass produce cars and other products. As a result, workers moved from rural areas to large cities to work in the factories. The rapid urbanization of the population led to radical changes in life styles and in the role of various members of society.

Before this change old folks were able to continue making contributions to the family livelihood. However, urban lifestyle placed them in a different position. Factory owners and work supervisors preferred younger, faster, and more agile employees. Their goal was to produce as many pieces as possible in the shortest period of time. They did not need the experience of the elderly nor their advice. These changes left the elderly with nothing to do and no vital role to play in their urban, industrialized society. Thus, the concept of retirement arose more due to the fact that the elderly were not needed than to any conscious choice on the part of the elderly themselves. In addition, moving to the city had also ruptured the close-knit family groups of rural areas. Contrary to the typical rural pattern the urban elderly found themselves with no job, no income, and no near-by family to provide care.

At the same time a second evolution was taking place in our society. This change involved the relationship of the individual and the government. Prior to the Great Depression of the twentieth century Americans were fiercely proud and independent. They felt responsible for themselves, and anyone forced to go on the "dole" was looked upon as a failure. Dole recipients were either incapable, or they failed to put forth the necessary effort to provide for their own needs. However, during the Great Depression huge numbers of hungry, willing workers desperately sought non-existent work. The fact that they and their families were starving was not their fault. If the cause was not individual, it must be societal or economic. Certainly, the issue was much larger and more complex than the previously simple one of people failing because they did not know how to work or did not want to work. The gradually accepted premise was that since individuals could not solve their problems alone, the government must intercede on their behalf and that of millions of other individuals who were also suffering due to circumstances beyond their control. The result was that the Roosevelt administration began to institute programs to alleviate the economic hardships of the people. In a famous freedom speech FDR proclaimed two additional freedoms that were the right of every American: the freedom from fear and the freedom from want. Of course, these freedoms became the responsibility of an ever growing government, especially the latter.

This shift in attitude was, and is, certainly understandable given the economic deprivations of the Great Depression. Something had to be done, and the government seemed to be the only segment of society large enough and with enough power to resolve the problems and to reduce the economic hardships prevalent throughout the country. In addition, the humanitarian goal was certainly laudable. What a wonderful world it would be if everyone was free from fear and free from want. Government can provide assistance in two different and distinct ways. First, they can change policy in such a way as to promote private solutions to problems. Second, they can appropriate government funds collected from the taxpayers to alleviate the problems. The first type of assistance is indirect; the second is direct. The first costs little public money, if any; the second requires huge amounts of taxpayer money. The first involves no taxes; the second depends on tax revenues or debt. Of course, from a political point of view the negative factor related to programs that promote private enterprise solutions is that politicians do not get the credit; therefore, they do not incur the gratitude and allegiance of their constituents, which may cost them votes in the future.

Many of the measures enacted by the Roosevelt administration involved the expenditure of the people's money to solve problems identified by government politicians and bureaucrats. If people did not have work, the administration created federal job corps to put people to work. If the price of hogs was too low because there were too many hogs, it paid the farmers to kill them. However, in order to pay some people, the government had to take money away from other people. The result over the years of this expanding process has been a rapid rise in the amount of tax revenues the government must have in order to pay for all its now many, many programs to assist one segment or another of the economy, one group or another of the populace. This steady rise is often overlooked due to the tendency when contemplating government programs to consider only the money distributed to various groups without taking into account the source of the funds.

Where Does The Money Come From?

Few people consider or question the source of government funds. They view "Uncle Sam" as a kind and compassionate soul who has the money to give to those in need. In fact, the current position of many recipient groups in our society is that they are "entitled" to government support, financial and otherwise. However, "Uncle Sam" has no money. Government does not produce wealth. Only investors, creators, and workers are producers. They indeed create wealth. Government only consumes wealth or transfers it from producers to non-producers. The bureaucrats charge for their services, of course, thus consuming part of the taxes they collect from the producers. In addition, they take part of the wealth that producers create and give it to others who are consumers of that created wealth. Of course, the lines between producers of wealth and consumers of wealth become rather blurred due to the fact that in modern society many people are both a producer and a contributor to government funds while at the same time being both a recipient of and consumer of government monies. The reader should keep this economic reality in mind while thinking about the role of government in all the Social Security programs.

Where does the money come from? Taxes. In 1940 few people paid income taxes. James Dobson tells of finding one of his father's check stubs from 1949. That year his father had earned $60.00 a week, and his weekly state and federal taxes were $2.70. His yearly salary was $3,120.00, which was the median income for workers in the United States. Income taxes amounted to 2% of his salary, and total withholding was only 4.5% leaving him 95.5% of his earned income to support himself and his family and to save for the future. By 1994 the situation had undergone a remarkable transformation. The average family with children paid 37.6% of income for local, state, and federal taxes, which amounted to $10,060.00 per year, more, as Mr. Dobson points out, than the annual cost of the average home mortgage. (Dobson)

Of course, the cost to support all the social programs adopted by Congress has continued to rise. According to Senator Nichols of Oklahoma, by 1999 taxpayers making at least $25,000.00 per year, not the income of a rich person by any means, were paying 43.3% of their salary in federal income, Medicare, and Social Security taxes. When one considers that each of us must also pay a multitude of state and local taxes, it becomes frightfully clear that most of us work a large percentage of the year for the government in order to make it possible for the government to take care of us.

Each year the National Taxpayer's Union publishes the tax free date for the year. Although the actual date varies from worker to worker and state to state, most American workers must work for the government, which gets its share first, the first five to six months of each year. In 2014 tax freedom day was April 21st, which was 3 days later than in 2013, which was 5 days later than in 2012. (www.usgovernmentspending.com)

The change has been dramatic in the last fifty years. As the American people have tended toward a greater and greater rejection of personal responsibility, the government has assumed more and more, and taxes have risen higher and higher to pay the incurred costs. The irony is that the public has grown to expect and to depend upon government expenditures, but they dislike paying the high taxes to support the payments. In a 1994 Wall Street Journal/NBC poll 61% of the respondents felt that entitlement payments should be decreased to reduce the federal deficit. However, 66% of the same group rejected the possibility of cutting Social Security, Medicare, Medicaid and farm subsidies (Thomas). Fred Goldberg, former commissioner of the Internal Revenue Service, appraises the rising costs of entitlements as follows: "If we do nothing, we will be required to double every single tax, or we will be required to cut every single benefit in half, by the year 2030." (Thomas).

What Possibilities Exist For Funding Retirement?

In this section we will assume that all workers have the freedom to choose any option regarding the funding of their own retirement, and based on that assumption, we will examine fictitious examples of some of the various possibilities.

Joe is eighteen. Having just graduated from high school, he now has his first job. His immediate necessity and primary goal is saving enough money to make the down payment on a new car. His secondary goal is to have a good time, especially with a fun-loving young lady who has attracted his fancy. Essentially, Joe settles into a life of living for the moment giving no thought to the future and to his money needs after he no longer has a job.

Joe through his own lack of foresight and personal responsibility has committed his later years to the care of others. If friends and family do not support him, some government agency will have to do so. He himself will have made no contributions. Taxpayers will have to bear the burden of his financial needs after he is no longer able to work. By failing to take responsibility for himself, he has committed himself to living on welfare after retirement.

Mary is not so irresponsible as Joe. She realizes that the elderly need money on which to live and that she, too, will need money when she stops working in her later years. Therefore, she is willing to give part of her earnings as a teacher to help provide retirement support for an older neighbor. Of course, her contribution alone is not sufficient to allow her neighbor to live comfortably. Other workers also contribute to his upkeep. All do so under the assumption that when they retire neighborly workers at that time will do the same for them.

Mary has chosen a support system in which her contributed funds are transferred immediately to a retiree.

This type of retirement funding is called a "pay-as-you-go" system because the money moves almost immediately from workers to retirees. A "pay-as-you-go" system is essentially a non-funded system in the sense that money being received is paid out when received as opposed to being saved and invested for future needs.

Beth is a lawyer. She is also willing to contribute a portion of her earnings to help meet the needs of workers currently retired. The difference between her program and that of Mary is that she does not give her money directly to a retiree. Instead, she gives it to someone charged with distributing it to retirees. However, she does so with the expectation that she will receive money from the same source when she retires.

The primary difference between Mary's program and Beth's is one that is not overtly obvious to the contributors and the recipients. In the latter retirement system one of the goals is to distribute the collected funds according to the needs of the recipients regardless of their past contributions to the program. In this case, Beth, who had high earnings as a lawyer and thus contributed more, will receive a smaller percentage of her salary during her retirement years while someone with low earnings will receive a higher percentage.

Matthew is in business. He is acutely aware of the costs and rewards of using money to create wealth. Part of his character and his career is to invest now in order to profit later. He regularly places a percentage of his earnings into an investment account to grow in anticipation of his retirement.

Matthew has chosen to put aside money that he hopes will grow into a sizable sum to pay for his retirement. His money and whatever it earns are his when he chooses to withdraw them from his account and to spend it for his needs during his non-working years. His is a "funded" program in the sense that funds exist that he may withdraw to provide economic support during his retirement.

Melvin is an adventurous fellow. He likes excitement. His focus is on his next planned escapade, whether it be tubing down a local river or rafting down the Colorado. Like Joe, he rarely gives any thought to matters such as how he will live after retirement. However, one day when he is in his fifties, the thought occurs to him that being able to retire at sixty in order to have more time to play golf and to travel would be wonderful. He likes the idea, but he has no money in savings to support his desires. Looking around for some way to make a lot of money quickly, he discovers an investment plan in which the promised return is an amazing twenty percent, exactly the type of program that he needs. He begins to put every extra dollar that he can save into the program.

All goes well. Melvin is quite pleased with the returns on his investment, so well pleased, in fact, that he places the profits as well as new money into the plan. He continues to put everything he has into the program and to dream about retirement. His dreams burst, however, when he learns to his sorrow that he has been investing in a Ponzi scheme. (A Ponzi scheme is one in which the manager or director of the scheme uses funds from new investors to pay supposed earnings on funds previously invested by previous participants. Obviously, when new funds cease, the entire scheme collapses from a lack of revenue to pay earnings because there were never any earnings.) He suddenly loses all his money. Broke, he, like Joe, will have to depend upon welfare for support during retirement.

Obviously, these fictitious examples are chosen to represent various possibilities for taking care of the elderly when they no longer have jobs and even if they have no family to care for them. The first, fourth, and fifth are impossible in most cases because under the laws of the 1983 Amendments to Social Security practically all workers, including the self-employed, have to make payments to Social Security. In addition, private Ponzi schemes are illegal.

Workers like Matthew may establish their own private program. However, they must also contribute to Social Security. Private retirement programs by law must be fully funded. Given the fact that Social Security is a non-funded, "pay-as-you-go" system, it is
similar to the fictitious programs in which Mary and Beth participate. However, one of the major features of Social Security is that it is redistributive, i. e., low wage earners receive a higher percentage of their contributions in

retirement than high wage earners. Therefore, of the five examples Social Security is most like the third. An additional and important aspect of Social Security is that benefits are indexed to inflation. As the cost-of-living index rises so, too, do the benefits that retirees receive.

What is the Best Way to Provide Economic Support During Retirement?

The necessity of establishing a sound, workable, sustainable system of financial support for workers after retirement is obvious. Members of our society can not return to agrarian times in which the elderly continued to work with their family nearby to care for them when they were too old to care for themselves. Nor would one suggest or advocate leaving the elderly without a financial plan for their later, non-working life.

The discussion does not revolve around supporting or not supporting retirees but around 1. the institution of a sustainable program and 2. whether a government program, a private program, or a combination of the two would be best for recipients, for the economy, for society, and for the political process.

What Are Some Of The Problems Associated With Social Security?

The greatest, and fatal, weakness of the present Social Security system is that it is based on unsound economic principles. A "pay-as-you-go", non-funded program makes no provision for putting money aside now to pay out later to future retirees. Money contributed by current workers is distributed to current retirees. No monies are accumulated. Ozawa questions the fairness of such a system. Is it fair to require future workers to pay to fulfill an obligation that they had no voice in approving? Some people object. Dogan states, "One of the most obvious symptoms of resistance to the social security system is the rise of the

underground economy everywhere . . . The underground economy, moonlighting, tax-evasion, . . . the brain drain, the decline of the work ethic are so many perverse effects of excessive taxation, which finally impoverishes the community
as a whole even if it does reduce inequalities." (Dogan)

The present Social Security system is not sustainable indefinitely. In an aging society as the number of retirees increases in relation to the number of workers, the amount of money needed to fulfill previously-made commitments, i. e. promises made in the past, increases while the amount of money flowing into the system decreases. In 1945, there were 41 workers paying into the Social Security Trust Fund for each retiree drawing money from the fund. By 1965 that ratio had dropped to 4 to 1. It was 2.9 to 1 in 2012. It is expected to drop to 2 to 1 by 2030. The Social Security program is stable at a ratio of 3 to 1. Below 2 to 1 it is economically unsustainable. (de Rugby)

In addition, over the years politicians have steadily voted to cover larger numbers of workers until coverage is now almost universal, which in the beginning brings more money into the system but later adds to the number of recipients. Another problem related to the solvency of the system is that life expectancy has continued to rise while at the same time the tendency has been for workers to retire at an earlier age. The declining birth rate, which lowers the number of future workers, and the bulge of "baby boomers" moving toward retirement add to the financial strain on the system. Complicating the threat to the future solvency of the system has been the past tendency of the politicians to expand benefits as well as coverage (Ozawa, 135-6). Disability was added in 1954. Medicare became an entitlement program in 1965. SSI became part of the system in 1972. A drug benefits program was added in 2003. Furthermore, the economies of most industrialized societies in the Western World are plagued by high unemployment including a troublesome trend toward large numbers of long-term unemployed (Haanes-Olsen 14).

Notwithstanding the constant barrage of propaganda to convince them otherwise, young Americans seem intuitively to realize that the present Social Security system is moving steadily toward collapse or a radical reduction in benefits. The results of a recent poll indicate that among those under 35 almost half believe that they will receive no benefits. Only 9% think that they will receive the same benefits as today's retirees. Among the entire surveyed sample 29% do not expect to receive any benefits. Another 37% think that benefits will be reduced. The economic facts speak for themselves in spite of politicians' promises to the contrary. A further complication to the lack of adequate funding to pay for future retirees is that members of Congress have regularly raided any surplus funds in the Social Security system to pay for other government needs. When the government budget director maintained that the Social Security Trust Fund would continue to grow until 2025 in spite of the fact that paid benefits began to surpass collected Social Security taxes in 2010, Charles Krauthammer replied, "The Social Security trust fund is a fiction. . . . In other words, the Social Security trust fund contains . . . nothing." (Matthews)

One of the major arguments made against making changes to the current Social Security system is that one can never rely on the income of other types of investments for future retirement while the Social Security program is safe. However, when one considers that statement carefully, the facts indicate that they are not safe. First, payments to future retirees are not assured due to the fact that it is an unsustainable "pay-as-you-go" system. (Current predictions are that disability will run out of funds in 2016, Medicare in 2030, and Social Security in 2033.) In addition, there is no money in the fund. Past contributions have been replaced by government IOUs because politicians have "borrowed" the money to cover current governmental expenditures. Furthermore, the return on the money workers are required by law to put into Social Security is low for most workers, and even negative in some cases. (For example, an average two-income family with children will pay $320,000.00 into Social Security and expect to receive, if it is still solvent, $450,000.00 if they retire at 67. If they were to put $320,000.00 into a tax-deferred IRA over the years they could expect to receive $975,000.00. Even worse, a low-income male will actually receive less money in retirement than he paid into the system. The return for low-income blacks is even lower although they receive a higher rate of return because their life expectancy is shorter.) (www.heritage.org) And finally, there is no guarantee that payees into the system will ever receive any money in return   for their contributions. That is not part of the law, and the Supreme Court has ruled that the government is not obligated to pay them anything. In the words of Davies and Harrigan, "While the law requires Social Security to invest its surplus in Treasury Bills, the law does not require Social Security to give taxpayers their money back."

    The present system works as long as the number of contributors in relation to the number of recipients is large, as long as production is increasing, as long as wages are rising, and as long as inflation is low. When any of these necessary conditions do not exist, both short-term liquidity and long-term solvency are at risk. In such situations, which occur regularly in any economy, members of Congress raise Social Security taxes to compensate for the inevitable short-fall in the funds. The following table indicates clearly how rapidly the tax rates for Social Security have risen since 1970:

Year	Annual maximum taxable earnings (dollars)	Contribution rate (percent of taxable earnings) Employers and employees, each		
		OASDI	HI	Total
1940	3,000	1.00		2.00
1950	3,000	1.50		3.00
1955	4,200	2.00		4.00
1960	4,800	3.00		6.00
1965	4,800	3.62		7.24
1970	7,800	4.20	0.60	9.60
1975	14,000	4.95	0.90	11.70
1980	25,900	5.08	1.05	12.26
1985	39,600	5.70	1.35	14.10
1990	48,600	6.20	1.45	15.30

(Aaron, Bosworth, and Burtless)

OASDI = Old-Age Survivors and Disability Insurance
HI = Hospital Insurance

Although the tax rate has not increased in percentage terms since 1990, the amount of income upon which Social Security taxes are paid has steadily risen. The annual maximum taxable earnings in 2013 totaled $113,700.00. As has been true historically, that figure will be temporary in all likelihood.

The present Social Security system is legal because it is a government program. If it were private, the same type of program would be illegal because it is unfunded and the money collected is not invested. Ponzi schemes and "pay-as-you-go" programs have been rightly declared illegal because they are not fiscally sound. They are banned in order to protect people's savings and to prevent their participating in financial schemes that are doomed to failure.

The use of the term "social security" is inappropriate. It does not, and was never intended to, ensure "social security". The original intent was to supply a minimum income to retirees who were moved out of the work force due to industry requirements.

The purpose was always "financial" rather than "social". Of course, no one, not even the government can guarantee "social" security, which consists of many factors in addition to the financial. And with regard to security, whether receiving a minimum income for life after retirement qualifies as "security" depends upon one's definition of the term. Obviously, what constitutes "security" varies from one individual to another.

"Financial assistance" or "minimal financial assistance" would have been more precise and more truthful terms than "social security". (It is also interesting to note that when Social Security became law in 1935 the average life expectancy was 61.9, 3.1 years below the retirement age. The average person was not expected to live to collect Social Security retirement! If the same ratio had remained in effect over the years, today's workers would not be eligible to retire and receive Social Security until around age 80!) (www.answers.yahoo.com)

The present Social Security system entices the current generation to take the money and enjoy the benefits with little or no thought as to the financial burden the resultant obligations are placing on future generations.

In our society we are often encouraged to buy now and to pay later. Social Security is the government version of that system. Present contributors support current recipients with the expectation that their benefits will be paid by future workers who had no voice in making the commitment. In addition, their burden will be heavier than that of the current generation because costs are rising dramatically and are projected to continue doing so. Parents would not consider contracting debts with the thought that their children would have to pay them, but we are involved in a similar transfer of obligation by our highly-favored and widely-supported Social Security system.

The present system allows politicians to buy votes with the promise of additional benefits to be paid for by future generations. The pattern has been a history of ever-expanding programs and ever-increasing costs. Repeatedly the result has been a financial crisis in the system, and repeatedly the politicians have raised taxes to maintain the liquidity and the solvency of the program. As Dogan observes, "It is easier to increase taxation for social security by 1 or 2 percent every year than in any way to limit the benefits." He adds that in Italy one in ten are "unfit for work", including forty percent of their former parliamentarians (Dogan). The cost of the various Social Security programs including old-age, disability, and hospitalization insurance has grown steadily.

In a "pay-as-you-go" system like Social Security workers proceed through the system, and through life, in two phases. First, they work and contribute a portion of their wages to the system. Second, they retire and receive monthly benefits from the system.

Each generation passes through in a two-step fashion. First they pay in order to support the previous generation; they are in turn supported by the pay of a succeeding generation of workers. At least that is how the system works in theory. In practice, circumstances may arise in which the funds coming into the system are not sufficient to meet the committed obligations. Genetski maintains, "Social Security is a ticking bomb. By taxing a large part of a worker's income and promising "security," the system reduces the worker's ability and incentive to save and hinders long-term growth." (Genetski)

Payment of payroll Social Security taxes is compulsory for most workers. There is no alternative, no recourse. They contribute a portion of their wages, and their employer contributes an equal amount. The money comes out of workers' checks before they receive them. Employers must factor the Social Security taxes into their labor costs.

Present participants in Social Security have no choices. One plan is available for everyone. There are no variations. They can not choose how much to contribute, how their contribution will be used, when they must retire, nor how much they can earn after they retire. Retirement at a specified age is mandatory, if the participant wishes to receive his full retirement benefits.

Built into the Social Security system of benefits is a redistributive factor, which means that money is transferred from one group to another. This redistribution is both intragenerational and intergenerational. It is intragenerational in the sense that low-wage earners receive a larger percentage of their income in retirement than high-wage earners. It is intergenerational in the sense that up to this point in the history of the system present participants have paid higher payroll taxes than the previous generation, and members of the future generation are scheduled to pay more than those of the present generation. That is, one group of workers contributes money that is redistributed to another group in order to equalize economic benefits. This redistribution involves a movement of funds from the rich to the poor, the younger to the older, and, in the case of health insurance, from the healthy to the sick. For example, in 1983 in France seventy percent of the social security budget was spent on ten percent of the insured (Dogan 49).

The regulations of the present Social Security system impose a penalty on workers who are willing and able to work beyond the mandatory retirement age. According to this "earnings test", those who work while receiving Social Security benefits have their payments reduced by one dollar for every three dollars they earn, which is in effect a 33% tax on each dollar earned beyond the annual amount exempted. (The "test" does not apply to sources of income other than employment.)

The present Social Security system encourages dependence upon government programs and discourages individual responsibility and initiative. Participants do not have to practice frugality. They do not have to plan for the future. They have "social security" to take care of that aspect of their lives. For example, workers tend to retire at an earlier age under the Social Security system than had been the case previously. In 1960 over thirty-three percent of the men over 64 were still employed while that number had dropped to sixteen percent by 1985. The number of beneficiaries increased from 3,477,243 in 1950 to 14,844,589 in 1960 to 26,228,629 on the way up to 50,898,244 in 2008 with a payout of $615,344 million dollars. In addition, there were 7,529,501 people drawing money from SSI, a total of $43,040 million. In 1940 of 9 million people over 65 two million were working and two million were on welfare. By 1980 thirty-two million retirees, dependents, and survivors were receiving benefits from OASI (Wachter 72-73).

The present Social Security system leads to decreased savings among individuals in society. There is no longer any need to save for the future, to have extra money in some safe place to cover their needs for a rainy day. Unemployment is covered. Disabilities are covered. Health is covered. Old age is covered. Nor is saving possible in many cases due to the high levels to which compulsory payroll taxes have risen. The result is a savings rate too low to fund needed investments to increase production and jobs. For example, in 1977 the amount of money, i. e., savings, needed to create one new job ranged from $20,000.00 to $70,000.00 (Calvert). U. S. citizens save 5.8% of their income. Of course, the savings rate correlates generally with the tax rate, although in countries like Belgium people save in spite of high taxes. In Spain and Portugal the tax rate is low, and the savings rate is high. In ten countries the savings rate is above ten percent with a high of 19.1% in Ireland. (Sauter, et al.)

So far foreign investors have been willing to fund our deficits, the result of which has been to convert the U. S. from a creditor nation to a debtor nation. Of course, the willingness of foreign investors to subsidize our debt is ependent upon the general health of the economy, and the question remains as to how healthy any economy can be that depends upon foreign capital for its funding. As Michael J. Boskin says, ". . . there is no convincing example in economic history of an advanced economy financing its long-term development by continuing to rely on foreign capital to finance its investment." (Wachter). Arthur J. R. Smith addresses the connection between savings and jobs saying, "The implications . . . are starkly clear: if we do not make room for . . . high savings and financial flows to new investment, there is no way to create new jobs at an adequate rate." (Calvert). Martin Feldstein, Harvard economist, "has estimated that the establishment and expansion of the non-funded Social Security system has reduced by 30%--50% the incentive of private persons to save, and hence has cut deeply into the base of normal capital formation, seriously slowing the growth of the American economy in comparison with those of other leading industrial nations." (Calvert).

The present system is paternalistic. The implication is that workers will not prepare adequately during their working years for their financial needs during their non-working years. Therefore, the government must institute a one-for-all compulsory program to require them to do so for their own good. Many proponents of Social Security consider it to be a "merit good".

The present system contains many inequities. The replacement percentage, i. e., the amount of pre-retirement income received after retirement, is higher for some participants than for others. Because of the fact that they live longer women receive more money over their retirement lifetime than men. The system subsidizes the traditional family structure in that homemakers are eligible to draw in benefits a certain percentage of their working spouses' benefits even though they were never employed outside the home. Since low-income workers tend to have a shorter life span than high-income workers, they do not receive as much money in retirement. Future generations of workers will pay higher Social Security payroll taxes but receive lower relative benefits than current retirees. Those who are able to wait to start collecting benefits until after they are 67 and wish to do so will receive higher monthly payments (Wolff). Although past participants have received benefits much, much larger than their past contributions would warrant, this largess diminishes as the system ages, and the return to some future participants will be negative, i. e., they will receive less than they have contributed. In 1986 the rate of return was 3.74% for low income wage earners, 2.3% for average wage earners, and 1.95% for high wage earners, a statistic which led Blinder to comment, "Obviously, no private, voluntary pension plan could redistribute income in this way, for the rich would simply opt out." (Wachter). Ferrara lists the real rates of return on Social Security payroll taxes as ranging from -1.5% for a single maximum-income worker to +2.75% for low-income worker with a non-working spouse. Of the twelve family combinations calculated the real rates of return are negative for four, zero for two, and positive for six, although the real rates of return for all combinations are much lower than one would expect from funds invested in the private sector of the economy over a worker's lifetime. Converted into dollars and cents, these percentages are much more alarming. For example, for individuals age 55 in 1983 all workers in all family situations will receive more on the average from Social Security than they have paid into the system except for unmarried males making above $15,00.00 per year. Those making $35,700.00 will receive $21,509.00 less than they have paid into the system.

Contrasting that figure with the corresponding figures for workers age 25 in 1983 reveals the difference between the benefits that older workers have received and those that younger workers will receive. All workers age 25 in 1983 making $35,700.00 will receive less on the average in benefits than they have contributed to the system. The range is from $6,012.00 for a working husband making $35.700.00 per year to $80,175.00 for an unmarried male making $35,700.00 per year (Ferrara, 1985).

What Are the Projections of the Future of the Present Social Security System?

Given the large number of inherent problems associated with the present Social Security system, what will happen if the public continues to favor it and politicians continue to support it without making fundamental changes? Predictions vary. However, even assuming that the most optimistic conditions prevail continuously, contributions will not be adequate to fund all the legislated benefits.

Meyer foresees the following: Solvency for OASI for the next 25 years if economic conditions are such as to avoid high inflation, high unemployment, and declining real wages. HI is moving steadily toward insolvency. By the end of the decade Medicare will be running an annual deficit of 20 billion dollars per year. SMI costs will rise to 5% of taxable earnings. To fund all the expenditures of OASDHI will require 13.94% of payroll under the most optimistic projections up to 28.5% of payroll under the most pessimistic projections (Meyer).

In 1994 President Clinton appointed a Bipartisan Commission on Entitlement and Tax Reform requesting that they study ways 1. to reduce the budget deficit and 2. to promote investment and economic growth.

This Commission published their preliminary findings in a report titled "Draft Commission Findings". Their overall conclusion was that "A better future for America can be secured if the country embarks on the course of long-term reform." After analyzing all available data from a large number of government agencies dealing with entitlements, commission members published the following findings:

#1 Current Trends Are Not Sustainable

#2 Our Competitors Save and Invest More Than We Do

#3 Mandatory Spending in the Federal Budget Continues to Grow

#4 Federal Spending on Health Care is Projected to Triple by 2030

#5 An Aging Population Means Fewer Workers

To Support Each Retiree's Benefits

#6 Medicare HI is Projected To Be Insolvent by 2001 (That prediction was not correct. The current forecast is insolvency in 2026.)

#7 Social Security Tax Collections Exceed Current Benefits, But Aren't Enough to Fund Future Promises

Why are current trends not sustainable? The inescapable answer is that promised benefits exceed anticipated revenues. In 2013 direct revenues totaled $2,775.1 million.

Federal expenditures 2012 were $3,454.6 billion. The cost of the 79 means tested entitlement programs was $2,287,133 million. The climbing national debt was $17,738,908,557,000.00. (www.treasurydirect.gov)

What has happened to savings as the Social Security system has steadily increased the federal government's role in personal welfare? Since the 60s private saving has dropped from more than 8% to 5.8%. Meanwhile government deficits have generally increased. The federal deficit in 1940 was $2.9 billion. In 1950 it was $3.1 billion. In 1960 there was a $.3 billion surplus. In 1970 the deficit was 2.8 billion. However, the effects of the Great Society programs became evident in the deficit of $73.8 billion in 1980. By 1990 the government was in the red that year $221.2 billion climbing to a total of $1,294 billion in 2010. Although it did drop to a deficit of $492 billion in 2014 the cost of entitlements continues to rise. (www.davemanuel.com) In summary, the inescapable fact is that the lower individual savings rate correlates strongly with increasing federal deficits as government programs supply a greater and greater portion of individual needs.

What is the extent of mandatory spending? Expenditures for the Social Security, health care, welfare, and interest on the national debt now account for more than 67% of the federal budget, which leaves little to pay for other components in the federal budget. What are the projected costs of health care? Costs for health care have been rising at more than 10% annually for the last five years. Current predictions are that Medicare and Medicaid will run out of funds in 2030. (Curry)

What changes are predicted to occur in our society? By 2030 there will be approximately two people of working age for each retiree. The result will be higher Social Security costs, which will rise from approximately 8% of the economy to 14%.

What will happen to the costs of Medicare? The public trustees of the Medicare Hospital Insurance (HI) program predict that it will be insolvent by 2026. Unless changes are made in the funding and the benefits, Medicare HI costs will increase to 8% of the payroll tax base while funding will remain around the current 3%. With regard to Medicare Supplementary Medical Insurance (SMI), currently beneficiaries pay 25% of the cost with 75% coming from general revenues. The trustees project that SMI costs will rise from the current 1% of the payroll tax base to more than 7% by 2030.

What are the estimates with regard to the imbalance between scheduled Social Security revenues and legislated benefits? By 2013 the outflow for benefits will exceed incoming revenues. The projection is that the trust fund will become bankrupt in 2033. Expenditures will consume approximately 17% of the payroll tax base while revenues will remain around 13% of the payroll tax base.

What Are Some of the Advantages of Replacing the Present Social Security System?

Replacing the present Social Security system with one based on sound economic principles, i. e., one that is fully funded, would improve the economic security of senior citizens, i. e., they would receive more money during retirement and have their accumulated capital left for their heirs if they so desired. In a funded program, money set aside by workers for their own use after retirement does not depend upon the willingness or ability of future generations of workers to fulfill commitments made by workers of previous generations. The money is available. The workers put it there. It belongs to them. Ferrara has prepared comparison tables showing the difference between the income that various family combinations would receive from a private, funded personal retirement account at different rates of return and that of the present Social Security system. (Due to space limitations only one family combination is presented here. The author encourages interested readers to study the tables in the book.)

The career minimum-wage earner with a non-working spouse is offered the best deal from social security. But through the private system, such a worker could still retire with accumulated assets of $275,243.00. Annual returns alone would pay the worker and his spouse $16,515.00 each year in benefits, about 75 percent more than the social security benefits of $9,354.00 with both alive and 2.5 times the program's benefits of $6,236.00 with one alive, all the while allowing them to leave one-quarter million dollars to their children or other heirs. Alternatively, worker and spouse could receive a life annuity paying about 2.5 times what social security would pay (Ferrara).

A personal retirement fund would encourage individual workers to build up as much wealth as possible. The choice would be theirs. They would have the opportunity to use their extra money to earn more money for their own use after retirement. Genetski presents the following example. If a twenty-year old worker puts 11.2% of his $20,000.00 income each year into a retirement account, if it earns 6% a year, if he never gets a raise during his lifetime, and if he retires at age 67, he will have accumulated $575,000.00 to do with as he wishes with no strings attached. (Genetski)

A personal retirement fund would permit all workers to retire when they chose and to use the money as they would like. The money would be theirs, and they could make the decision as to when they might like to begin drawing from their accumulated funds and in what manner. In addition, there would be no strings attached as to whether they could continue to work while drawing the money from their personal fund. There would be no justification for government deductions or penalties.

Millions of personal retirement funds in the nation's banking system would create huge pools of money for investment to fund new enterprises and to create new jobs.

With such a large amount of capital available interest rates would be lower, economic growth would be greater, and the current American dependence on foreign capital would be less. Calvert points out one of the benefits of a private funded system saying, "The reserves set up by the funded plans do many things besides providing pensions. They also provide the capital that the economy needs to generate production." (Calvert) Genetski describes the positive change that occurred in Chile when workers were given the option of establishing personal savings accounts for retirement. Workers putting money into their personal retirement accounts resulted in a savings rate of 29% which in turn funded an economic growth rate of close to 7% annually. The author concludes, "Instead of resenting the rich, Chile's workers themselves are becoming rich." (Genetski)

The institution of personal retirement accounts would encourage individual responsibility and resourcefulness with regard to planning and saving for retirement. Workers' choices would be their own. They would make the decisions influencing their retirement.

Having personal retirement funds unencumbered with a complex set of regulations would enable workers to retire at the time and under the circumstances they would select. Some might choose to retire early while others might prefer to continue pursuing a productive life as long as their emotional, physical, and psychological health permitted. Leaving the decision regarding the age of retirement to each individual would enable people to work as long as they would like. Tapping the incredible experience, expertise, energy, desire, and good will of the elderly would make a significant addition to the nation's resources. The forced idleness of millions of capable individuals is unwise as well as wasteful. As Benjamin Franklin reflected, "There is nothing wrong with retirement as long as one doesn't allow it to interfere with one's work." Calvert presents a number of examples of individuals who made major contributions to civilization after the age of sixty-five. Michelangelo, for example, began to re-plan the capitol in Rome the year he reached sixty-five. Six years later he designed and began work on the construction of St. Peters in Rome. At age eighty he completed the Pieta, one of the greatest sculptures in the history of art. Winston Churchill took control of the defense of England in World War II shortly after reaching the normal retirement age. Even Prince Bismarck of Germany, who instituted the world's first social insurance program of financial support for those who retire from work at age sixty-five, did not retire at that age. In fact, he introduced the program when he himself was sixty-eight, and he continued performing his duties running the German government until he was seventy-five (Calvert).

Permitting and encouraging the elderly to continue working part time or in less strenuous situations would help restore a feeling of worth and usefulness in senior citizens. Productive work is not an evil to be shed at a certain age. It provides a sense of worth and importance that should not be discarded automatically or denied when someone reaches an artificially determined age. A high quality life is not synonymous with freedom from labor. In fact, just the opposite may be the case. Calvert observed, "The one great service provided by pension plans, the regular arrival of the monthly pension cheque, does nothing to meet many of the problems of aging." (Calvert). With regard to the basic human needs of all individuals, the same author quotes Lynda King Taylor, adviser to the Work Research Unit of the Department of Employment in Great Britain, who states, "There are three inborn needs--security, stimulation, and identity. The commonly experienced opposites are anxiety, boredom, and anonymity." (Calvert). Neither retiring from work nor receiving regular retirement checks eliminates those human needs nor the dreaded opposites. He also cites Dr. Hans Selye, a Canadian researcher who advises, "Man must work . . . We have to begin by clearly realizing that work is a biological necessity. Just as our muscles become flabby and degenerate if not used, so our brain slips into chaos and confusion unless we constantly use it for some work that seems worthwhile to us." He adds, "For many older people, the most difficult aspect of retirement to bear is the feeling of being useless . . . The continuous leisure of enforced retirement is certainly not an attractive way of life . . . Nothing to do is not rest; a vacant mind and a slothful body suffer the distress of deprivation . . . The fatal enemy of all utopias is boredom." (Calvert). Yet it is just this type of utopia of endless nothing to do that has been sold in modern industrialized societies as the ideal way to spend one's "golden years".

Shifting programs for funding retirement from the public treasury to individual accounts would eliminate a drain on the national treasury if and/or when funds have to be taken from the general fund to make mandated Social Security payments.

Removing retirement programs from the political arena would make it impossible for politicians either to assassinate their opponents by suggesting that they plan to change the Social Security system or to purchase votes by promising the voters some benefit to be paid for later by a succeeding generation, a sometimes irresistible temptation.

Personal retirement funds would be fiscally sound. Workers would put money into their own account. This money would be invested to create additional wealth for their use during retirement or for their heirs. The money would be secure, independent from unpredictable and uncontrollable future demographic changes or political events. The resultant funds would constitute a national resource of capital for the creation of wealth.

Instituting a system of personal retirement funds would eliminate current arbitrary rules of inequity. Since all workers would have their own fund, the accrued benefits would be theirs. All would receive according to their own contributions. Thus, the system would be fair to all.

Under a system of personal retirement funds the accumulated funds belong to individuals to do with as they want. Unencumbered by regulations requiring that they work until a specified age and penalties against working beyond a specified age, they would be free to work as long as they would like and to change jobs as they wished. If they wanted to lengthen their productive life, they would be free to do so. If they preferred the physical, psychological, emotional, and social stimulation of the workplace to a life of leisure in retirement, the decision would be theirs.

What Are Some Alternatives To Social Security?

The present OASI system is not the only way to provide economic security for the elderly. A serious examination of the goals of OASI and a complete analysis of the most effective and efficient programs for accomplishing those goals will surely stimulate the formulation of a number of possibilities. Ferrara describes three that have already been instituted.

Britain has a two tier system. The first is compulsory; the second is voluntary. All workers pay into the first and receive the same benefits regardless of wages earned during their working years. These benefits provide a minimum income during retirement. Benefits from the second correspond to earnings. The more workers earn the more they receive in retirement. The government grants a tax reduction for those who participate in the voluntary program, so contracting out of the system for this portion of their retirement is to their financial advantage. Workers participating fully in their social security system pay a payroll tax of 18.5% while those in the voluntary program pay 11.5% into the state system and 7.5% into their personal retirement account. By year five of the two-tier system forty-five percent of the workers was participating in the voluntary program. The result to the government was to reduce their future social security liability by over 30%.

In 1981 the Chilean government adopted a system of opting out of social security. Under the new program workers could put 10% of their income into IRA accounts managed by private companies. Those who chose to remain in social security paid a payroll tax of 27% while those who chose an IRA account paid 17%. The program has been extremely popular. Between May and December of 1981 over 50% opted out of the state-run system. All new workers are required to open a personal account rather than to participate in their social security system. (As reported elsewhere in this discussion, the beneficial effect of this private program led to a savings rate of 29% and an annual growth rate in the economy of over 7%.)

In an article in the New York Times John Tierney compared what his retirement benefits would be if he had participated in the Chilean system versus what it would be from Social Security. If he retired in ten years at age 62, he would have an annual pension of $55,000.00 with the Chilean retirement system versus $18,000.00 with Social Security. If he were to retire at 65 with the Chilean system, he would receive an annual pension of $70,000.00 versus $25,000.00 annually under Social Security. Another option he would have in Chile would be to retire with an annual pension of $53,000.00 per year and an initial lump sum payment of $223,000.00. (Tierney)

Officials and employees of the Baylor University Medical Center opted out of the Social Security system in 1982 to establish their own program. Their "integrated plan" provides retirement income equal to 60-65% of the employee's working wage plus survival and disability benefits. Retirees participate in Medicare if they are eligible. If not, Baylor pays equivalent benefits for its retirees. The cost is 8.4% of wages, which is considerably less than the Social Security payroll tax. Estimates are that the Center and its employees have saved 92 million dollars in ten years with their program. (Ferrara)

Recently, an investment expert recommended that parents put $10,000.00 into a variable annuity for each child at birth. Based on the traditional average annual return for stocks, he estimated that the child's account balance would be approximately one million dollars at age 65. Some system of setting up a personal account for each child would seem to be much simpler and would appear to provide a much larger return than the present OASI.

David Ranson presents the following criteria for reforming Social Security:

1. A redesigned social security system ought to restore, rather than further weaken, incentives to participate in the economy. He suggests that two ways to discourage work and production are 1. to impose a tax on earnings and

2. to enable people to live without working.

3. Present liabilities should be honored. However, future costs of the present system should not be a factor in the adoption of a new program.

4. The new system should be independent of politics.

5. Any new system should be simple and easy for participants to understand. Periodic reports should be made to participants.
6. The program should be self-financing and protected from financial threat.
7. Participants should be able to understand the formula and to calculate their future benefits.
8. The program should not subsidize one group at the expense of another.
9. Anyone would be permitted to opt out of the program. In case a large number did so, the program would be financially sound for the remaining participants.
10. All accounts would be funded. No new non-funded accounts would be permitted.
11. The program would impose no disincentives on work, production, savings, or investment (Ferrara, 1985).

What Can Be Done?

Converting the present "pay-as-you-go" public Social Security system to one that is funded will be extremely difficult. Social Security is a major component of our political system, of our economy, and of our society. Many past and current retirees are strongly in favor because their returns have been outstanding in the start-up phase of the program. One group, the National Committee to Preserve Social Security and Medicare, has 6 million members poised to attack anyone who suggests a critical evaluation of the system. Another, the AARP is constantly on the alert to protect its members' benefits (Thomas). Of course, for various reasons, including the need to be re-elected, most politicians feel that Social Security is better left untouched. Perhaps, Genetski overstates the case when he says, "The real objection to privatizing Social Security is that it would shift tremendous power and influence from politicians to individual workers." However, he has a point.

The key to change is education. If Americans understand that private, funded alternatives can lead to a stronger economy and to greater income during their retirement and if they convey that realization to their representatives, politicians will no longer be afraid to consider alternatives that would be better for the economy and for individual retirees than Social Security. Workers have to realize two things. First, the goal under any proposed alternative is to provide economic security during retirement. (Promises to past and current participants in Social Security must be met.) Second, they can have more money and more economic security in a funded system than in one that is non-funded. (Why should they settle for minimum or even negative future returns on their compulsory contributions to Social Security when personal IRA accounts offer the possibility of creating considerable personal wealth over the period of their working years?)

All Americans stand to gain with a private, funded retirement system, but they believe that they will lose because they think in terms of Social Security or nothing. They need to understand that better alternatives are possible and desirable because they are more beneficial. Rethinking the present funding system for retirement is to their advantage. They are the ones who are currently settling for less when they could be in a system that would give them more.

Selected References

Aaron, Henry J., Barry P. Bosworth, and Gary Burtless. Can America Afford to Grow Old? Washington, D. C.: The Brookings Institute, 1989.

Bipartisan Commission on Entitlement and Tax Reform. Draft Commission Findings. Washington, D. C.: United States Senate.

Brain, Charles M. Social Security at the Crossroads: Public Opinion and Public Policy. New York: Garland Publishing, 1991.

Bureau of Labor Statistics, U. S. Department of Labor. 15 July 2014.

Calvert, Geoffrey N. Pensions and Survival: The

Coming Crisis of Money and Retirement. Toronto: Maclean-Hunter Limited, 1977.

Curry, Tom. "Medicare fund insolvency date a bit further away than last year." NBC News, 31 May 2013.

De Rugy, Veronique. "How Many Workers Support One Social Security Retiree?" Mecatus Center, George Mason University, 22 May 2012.

Dobson, James C. Focus on the Family. Colorado Springs, Colorado: 6 August. 1994, 6.

Dogan, Mattei. "The social-security crisis in the richest countries: basic analogies." International Social Science Journal, 37 (1985): 47-61.

Ferrara, Peter J., ed. Social Security: Prospects for Real Reform. Washington, D. C.: Cato Institute, 1985.

Ferrara, Peter J. "America's Ever Expanding Welfare Empire." Forbes, 22 April 2011.

Genetski, Robert. "Privatize Social Security." The Wall Street Journal, 21 May 1993, A 12.

Haanes-Olsen, Leif. "Worldwide Trends and Developments in Social Security, 1985-87." Social Security Bulletin, 52 (1989): 14-26.

Matthews, Merrill, contributor. "What Happened to the $2.6 Trillion Social Security Trust Fund?" Forbes, 13 July 2011.

Meyer, Charles W., ed. Social Security: A Critique of Radical Reform Proposals. Lexington, Massachusetts: D. C. Heath, 1987.

Moore, Stephen. "The Growth of Government in America" www.fee.org. 1 April 1993.

Ozawa, Martha N. "The 1983 Amendments to the Social Security Act: The Issue of Intergenerational Equity." Social Work. 29 (1984): 131-7.

Rose, Nancy E. "Work Relief in the 1930s and the Origins of the Social Security Act." Social Service Review, 63 (1989): 63-91.

Sauter, Michael A., Charles B. Stockdale, and Douglas A. McIntyre. "The 10 Countries Where People Save the Most Money." Fox Business, 15 August 2011.

Tanner, Michael D. "Social Security: Follow the Math." www.cato.org. 14 January 2005.

"The World's Top-Saving Countries, 2013." <u>Forbes</u>, 8 November 2013.

Thomas, Paulette. "Bipartisan Panel Outlines Evils of Entitlements, But Hint of Benefit Cuts Spurs Stiff Opposition." <u>The Wall Street Journal</u>, 8 Aug. 1994, A 14.

Tierney, J. "The Proofs in the Pension." <u>New York Times</u>. 25 April 2005.

Wachter, Susan M., ed. <u>Social Security and Private Pensions: Providing for Retirement in the Twenty-first Century</u>. Lexington, Massachusetts: D. C. Heath, 1988.

Wolff, Nancy. <u>Income Redistribution and the Social Security Program</u>. Ann Arbor, Michigan: U-M-I Research Press, 1987.

www.answers.yahoo.com
www.bls.gov
www.davemanuel.com
www.en.wikipedia.org
www.heritage.org
www.ssa.gov
www.usgovernmentrevenue.com
www.usgovernmentspending.com
www.treasurydirect.gov

Rights Versus Entitlements:

What Are The Differences?

What Are The Consequences?

Jim Jones, his wife Sarah, and their two children are taking an afternoon stroll through their neighborhood. The sky is blue; the sun is shining. Jim and Sarah are chatting; the children are playing. Everyone is having a good time. All is peaceful. Suddenly, a police car screeches to a halt beside them. An officer jumps out and demands, "Get in the car. All of you. You are wanted at headquarters for questioning." Startled, Jim replies indignantly, "You can't do this to us. This is America. We have rights."

Is the officer's action appropriate? Is Jim's reaction justifiable? Do we have rights that neither government representatives nor others may violate? What is a right? Do we have natural rights? What rights are guaranteed by our Constitution? What are our unalienable natural rights?

Sam Smith, his wife Jane, and their two children live in a small, unkempt, fourth-floor apartment. Neither Sam nor Jane has a job. They exist on the government check that arrives monthly and the food stamps that they receive. One day they find in the mail a notice that all their current payments and food stamps will cease at the end of the month. Surprised, Sam replies indignantly, "They can't do that to us. This is America. We are entitled to food, shelter, and clothing."

Is the government's action appropriate? Is Sam's reaction justifiable? Are we entitled to receive food, shelter, and clothing from the government? What is an entitlement? To what government benefits are we entitled? What entitlements are guaranteed to us by our Constitution?

Rights

On July 4, 1776, representatives of the thirteen British colonies in North American adopted <u>The Declaration of Independence</u>. In the second and third paragraphs Jefferson boldly proclaims the justification for the declaration.

"We hold these truths to be self-evident, that all men are created equal, that they are endowed by their Creator with certain unalienable Rights, that among these are Life, Liberty and the Pursuit of Happiness. . . . That to secure these rights, Governments are instituted among Men, deriving their just powers from the consent of the governed . . ."

Clearly, Jefferson had four fundamental democratic principles in mind when he penned this powerful statement. First, all individuals are created equal. Second, they have God-given rights. Third, the purpose of government is to safeguard those rights for everyone. Fourth, politicians are representatives of the people, their power comes from the people, and they govern with the consent of the governed, who may withdraw that consent, as those who gathered to approve and sign <u>The Declaration of Independence</u> were doing. Jefferson's words are beguilingly simple, but the implications are remarkably profound. People have God-given rights, governments are to protect those rights, and the people control the government. What revolutionary ideas! What an ideal plan to maintain individual liberty! To those of us accustomed to living in a democracy these ideas seem natural and unquestionable. However, they were beyond the imagination of most people throughout history, and they are little more than a dream to many people in our contemporary world.

Long accustomed to freedom, we are likely to forget how extended and difficult the struggle for natural God-given rights has been. During most of recorded history those who were the most powerful or those who claimed divine right exercised control over the people and collected tribute from them. Dictators and kings never considered the rights of the people. In fact, except in those somewhat rare instances of a benevolent monarch, oppression of the masses was the rule. Indeed, rulers believed that what the people had was theirs and that in collecting taxes they were merely taking what rightfully belonged to them.

Several significant documents mark historical milestones in the slow evolution in the Western World toward individual rights. In 1215 a group of barons and church leaders forced King John of England to sign the Magna Carta in which he agreed to seek their advice and consent on matters of importance to the kingdom and to accept other articles which later became the basis for modern justice. In 1628 the English Parliament presented the Petition of Right to King Charles I in which they declared unconstitutional such acts as levying taxes without Parliament's consent, lodging soldiers in private homes, establishing martial law, and illegal imprisonment of citizens. In 1689 Parliament sent to King William III and Queen Mary a document specifying certain rights that were the "true, ancient, and indubitable rights and liberties of the people" that became known as the Bill of Rights. The American Bill of Rights, adopted in 1789 and ratified by the states in 1791, was included in the Constitution in the first ten amendments. The French adopted their Declaration of the Rights of Man and of the Citizen in 1789 guaranteeing freedom of religion, speech and the press as well as personal security. The United Nations adopted the Universal Declaration of Human Rights in 1948. The Canadian Parliament approved the Act for the Recognition and Protection of Human Rights and Fundamental Freedoms in 1960.

What are the God-given rights guaranteed in the various bills of rights? Although the wording varies from one to the other, there is remarkable agreement. All are designed to protect individual liberty.

The Canadian Bill of Rights provides an excellent example because of two paragraphs in the preamble and because of the simplicity of the statement of rights.

"The Parliament of Canada, affirming that the Canadian Nation is founded upon principles that acknowledge the supremacy of God, the dignity and worth

of the human person and the position of the family in a
society of free men and free institutions;

Affirming also that men and institutions remain free
only when freedom is founded upon respect for moral
and spiritual values and the rule of law; a) the right of
the individual to life, liberty, security of the person and
enjoyment of property, and the right not to be deprived
thereof except by due process of law;

a) the right of the individual to life, liberty, security
of the person and enjoyment of property, and the right not to
be deprived thereof except by due process of law;

b) the right of the individual to equality before the
law and the protection of the law;

c)   freedom of religion;

d)   freedom of speech;

e)   freedom of assembly and association; and

f)   freedom of the press."

A comparison of these bills of rights leads to several
obvious conclusions. Their purpose is to ensure freedom for
the individual. Although the implication is that their intent
is to protect the peoples' rights from any and all
infringement, their principle purpose is to protect the
individual from oppressive government. Their goal is to
make government subject to the people. Their justification
is that the delineated rights are God-given. Their
implication is that government has no authority to rescind or
to abuse these rights.

Entitlements

The concept of entitlements has a much shorter
history in the United States than does that of rights. In fact,
the word "entitlement" is listed as the noun form of "entitle"
in the first edition, 1969, of The American Heritage
Dictionary of the English Language. However, the editors of
the third edition, 1992, included an entry for "entitlement
program" defined as "A government program that guarantees
and provides benefits to a particular group."

Early settlers did not come to America to receive government benefits. They came to be free from government interference and to be free to pursue their own personal fulfillment. Aware of the potential for government tyranny and imbued with the Puritan work ethic, they were fiercely independent and strongly self reliant. They did not expect the government to take care of them. They did expect the government to guarantee their rights. They resisted any type of government assistance. In fact, those who did accept public payments, i. e., welfare, were described in pejorative terms as being on the "dole". In essence people on the "dole" were considered to be failures because the general belief was that in this great country of liberty and opportunity those who had the ability and the desire could succeed. The basis for success or lack of success lay with the individual. In most cases in which people could not provide for themselves, either permanently or temporarily, family, friends, or local churches provided for them. The few individuals who had no other means of support received assistance from local welfare agencies, including living on the "poor farm".

This general acceptance of individual responsibility changed for a significant segment of the population during the Great Depression. Until that point in our history people believed that the inability to achieve economic independence was the fault of the individual. However, in the early thirties thousands even millions of capable, hard-working men and women desperately searched for non-existent jobs. They and their families were starving, and the fault lay not in their inability or their unwillingness to work. There were no jobs available. If the fault was not theirs, the problem must be due to some other factor. If individuals could not correct the situation, some other larger entity such as the government should step in to solve the catastrophic economic problems that had paralyzed the nation. If people could not feed themselves and their family and if the fact that they could not do so was not their fault, well-meaning politicians were willing to assume that responsibility.

The economic and resultant social crisis of the Great Depression was exacerbated by the emergence of large centers of mass production during the latter part of the nineteenth and the early part of the twentieth centuries. Large numbers of people had left their family and friends to move to the big city to work in factories. The work was easier, and the pay was better. However, in doing so, they had abandoned the traditional security net that provided support during times of hardship. When the depression struck, no one was there to help them survive. Cramped into apartments and houses on small city lots, they did not even have the option of raising their own food. Where could they turn for support? Who would help them? The customary supportive structure no longer existed for many, and beginning with the Roosevelt administration in the early thirties agents of the government, elected and unelected, gradually began to assume greater and greater responsibility for taking care of citizens.

Providing benefits in the form of payments to individuals, i. e., entitlements, has grown steadily, especially beginning with Franklin Delano Roosevelt's first term and since passage of Lyndon Johnson's Great Society programs. For the most part the number of programs, the scope of the programs, the cost of the programs, and the number of recipients has increased consistently and persistently from that time to the present. Ferrara describes America's entitlement programs as ". . . a vast empire bigger than the entire budgets of almost every other country in the world." (2011)

However, in spite of the huge expenditures the intended reduction in poverty has not occurred. In fact, some would argue that poverty has worsened. Many scholars who study the economic, psychological and social aspects of poverty contend that this undesirable status is true with regard to economic conditions and that it is even more pronounced in the case of the psychological and social aspects of poverty. Good-hearted individuals at all levels of government have poured trillions of dollars into the war to eliminate economic poverty. However, the percentage of those in our country who are classified as being poor has changed very little, and their psychological and social plight is worse than their economic situation. Prior to the onset of impersonal government dependency poor people did not have money, but they were not poverty stricken personally or socially. Now, for many millions, dependency has become a persistent way of life from generation to generation.

Entitlement Spending

In 2011 the U. S. government had 79 means tested entitlement programs. The cash assistance program included SSI/Old Age, the earned income tax credit, the refundable child credit, the make work pay tax credit, the temporary assistance for needy families, foster care, adoptive assistance, refugee assistance, general assistance to Indians, and assets for independence at a total cost of $162,717 million. Medical programs included Medicaid, SCHIP, community health centers, maternal and child care, medical assistance to refuges, and healthy start at a total cost of $289,816 million. The food program included food stamps, the school lunch program, WIC, school breakfast, the child care food program, the nutritional program for the elderly, the summer program, the commodity supplement program, the temporary emergency food program, needy families, farmers' market nutrition, and special milk at a total cost of $102,288 million. Twelve programs in housing cost $54,058 million. Three programs in energy and utilities cost $6,403 million. Twelve programs in education cost $60,175 million. Ten programs in training cost $7,324 million. Thirteen programs in services cost $10,411 million. Four programs in child care and child development cost $15,961 million. Four programs in community development cost $7,937 million. The cost for the two major programs Social Security and Medicare was $785,000 million and $574,000 million respectively. The grand total for entitlement spending in the year 2011 was $2,287,133 million. (www.en.wikipedia.com)

For the fiscal year 2012 the federal government spent $3.54 trillion. The cost for Medicare and Medicaid was $802 billion or 23% of expenditures. Social Security cost $768 billion or 22% of the budget. The Defense Department spent $670 billion or 19% of the budget. Non-defense discretionary spending totaled $615 billion or 17% of the budget. Other mandatory spending totaled $461 billion or

13% of total expenditures. Interest payments on the national debt totaled $223 billion or 6% of the total budget. Federal expenditures were 22.8% of the nation's GDP. (www.en.wikipedia.com)

In 1900 government spending on entitlements was less than 1/2 of 1% of GDP. That figure was approximately the same in 1920. It rose to 3% by 1940. It was up slightly to 5% in 1960. After passage of the Great Society programs in 1965 expenditures on entitlement programs began to rise. In 1980 the cost of the numerous entitlement programs rose to 12% of GDP. In 2000 it was 13%, and the projection for 2015 is 17%. (www.usgovernmentspending.com)

The government spent very little on entitlements until the administration of FDR. Afterwards, entitlement spending was not a burden until 1965 and the institution of LBJ's Great Society. Government expenditures for pensions, health care, and welfare now constitute approximately 45% of the national budget, and predictions are that if entitlement expenditures continue to rise at the past rate they will consume the entire federal budget at some point in the future. (de Rugby) According to Robert Rector of the Heritage Foundation, by 2008 total welfare spending amounted to $16,800.00 per person and to $50,400.00 per family, which is more than enough to eliminate poverty, as Charles Murray points out in his book In Our Hands, A Plan to Replace America's Welfare State. (Ferrara). From 1968 to 1993, the first twenty-five years of the Great Society, the government spent $2.5 trillion dollars aiding the needy and the cities, which would have been enough money to buy all the farmland and all the Fortune 500 companies in the United States. (Moore, 1993) In 2013 over two thirds of government expenditures, 69.4%, were to pay for entitlement programs, which was up from 21.2% in 1962, which was up from 48.5% in 1990. (Muhlhausen and Tyrrell)

One example of the growth of entitlements is the rapid rise of people drawing disability benefits. Enrollment has skyrocketed in the last three decades, and especially during the administration of President Obama. The federal government now spends more on disability payments than on food stamps and welfare combined. In one county in Alabama one in four are on disability. Nine percent of the people in West Virginia are on disability. Nationwide the figure is 4.6%. The number of children on disability is seven times greater than thirty years ago. Many or most of these youngsters are subsequently doomed to doing poorly in school because if they improve and do well their parents lose their child's disability payments. (Joffe-Walt)

There are three major reasons for this enormous increase in the number of people on disability. The first is that going on disability is easy to do, and many take advantage of this perceived perk. The second is that disproving the applicant's testament of pain, or distress, or fatigue is difficult to ascertain and to disprove. The third is that in order to end "welfare as we know it", people were moved from welfare to disability. Since under this program welfare was the responsibility of the states and disability of the federal government, the states moved people from their payroll to that of the federal government. The State of Missouri, for example, paid agencies $2,300.00 per enrollee to enroll people in the federal disability program. One particularly enthusiastic Missouri law firm made $68.7 million dollars for their efforts. (Joffe-Walt)

The effects of the rising government funding requirements are multiple and complex, but one that is especially relevant to this discussion of retirement income and Social Security, or between individual responsibility for retirement support and that of the government, is that the government now requires so much of the workers' income that providing for their own retirement income has become increasingly difficult. Due to the perception that funding of retirement is the government's responsibility and to the fact that workers have less money after paying a large percentage of the income in taxes, Americans have a lower savings rate than do citizens of many other countries. The average savings rate in the U. S. is currently 5.8%. However, in ten countries it is over 10%. (Sauter, et al.)

Another effect of government spending to care for its citizens is the politicians' tendency to demand more control of the people and their life. That is, what they support they tend to want to control, and in order to control the people, they need to know what they are doing. Snyder summarizes the situation as follows: "Big brother is watching everything that you do on the internet and listening to everything that you say on your phone. Every single day in America, the U. S. government intercepts and stores nearly two billion emails, phone calls and other forms of electronic communication. . . . Many Americans may not realize this, but nothing that you do on your cell phone or on the internet will ever be private again." (Snyder)

In summary, providing economic independence for the elderly and the needy is a major commitment in our society. Given our modern, industrialized, urban society, the elderly are normally not welcome in the work force. In fact, they are encouraged not to work, and they may even be penalized if they do choose to work. In addition, they may not have the necessary family support to help them in times of difficulty. Given our expectations that government should provide a large number of entitlements and given our current tax system to pay for those entitlements, many workers do not have sufficient funds left over after paying taxes and after meeting their current needs to set aside anything for the future.

What Have Been The Results?

Franklin Delano Roosevelt envisioned an America in which its citizens would be free from fear and free from want. Lyndon Baines Johnson foresaw a Great Society funded by the wealth of America. Government policies favored by both presidents, and others who followed in their footsteps, have redistributed trillions of dollars from American taxpayers to the elderly and the needy. The intent was magnanimous, but inadequate to achieve the desired objectives. The expected utopia has not been achieved. The poverty rate, which was dropping prior to the institution of the Great Society programs, remains at approximately the same level as it was before the war on poverty.

Since the War on Poverty began fifty years ago the government has spent over $20 trillion dollars trying to lift people out of poverty. In spite of all that enormous sum of money 47 million people in America are still classified as poor. This situation exists in spite of the fact that half of all Americans receive a regular check from the government. ("Ending Welfare As We Know It")

Americans think of their country as one of wealth, and it is. However, many in our country still live below the poverty line, set by the government for 2014 at $23,850.00 for a family of four. In 2012 the poverty rate in America was 16%, including a 20% poverty rate for children. In 2013 UNICEF reported that the U. S. had the second highest poverty rate for children among all developed nations. In 2013 more than 43.6 million Americans were living below the poverty line, which was the highest level since 1993.

Since the 1980s the poverty rate in America has been higher than it is in many other wealthy nations. However, this group of people living in poverty tends to be somewhat fluid over a period of time. In fact, most Americans will be in poverty for a year or more between the ages of 25 and 75. (en.wikipedia.org) In 2014 one in six men between 25 and 54 was not working. Fifty years ago only one in twenty was not working. (Schlafly)

At what cost have government officials pursued this illusory dream? In the first place, the number of regulations has exploded as the politicians and bureaucrats have attempted to control the staggering number of programs in the entitlement system.

Federal regulations are divided into 50 broad areas. Each one contains one or more volumes. (www.gpo.gov) Fifty agencies attempt to understand and to enforce more than 150,000 pages of regulations. (Gattuso and Keen)

Two recent laws provide examples of how complex and cumbersome many of our laws have become. The Dodd-Frank Wall Street Reform and Consumer Protection Act runs to 2,319 pages. However, regulations must be added to that complex piece of legislation: 8,002 pages plus another 5,933 pages of proposed regulations. (Dodd-Frank: Four Years Of Failure")

The Affordable Care Act has approximately a thousand pages in the legislation plus 10,000 pages of rules and regulations. (A Rancid Stew Of Legislation")

In addition to federal regulations states, too, have their own plethora of rules and regulations. For example, the "Revised Code of Washington" is divided into 91 areas. One division, Fish and Wildlife is divided into 26 chapters which contain 39 sections. (www.heritage.org)

Of course, the purpose of federal regulations is to provide guidelines for administering all the many programs. However, entitlement programs not only lead to enormous numbers of rules and regulations; they also cost a lot of money. Obviously, to get the necessary funds, government must raise the money through taxation. (Just as customers pay higher prices for goods and services taxpayers provide the money that pays for all the entitlement programs. That is, some of the taxpayers do. In 2011 46.4% paid no federal income taxes. Furthermore, in that same year 30% of the workers who paid no federal income taxes actually qualified for an income tax credit and received money from the government.) (www.taxfoundation.org)

In order to pay for their many expenses the government has had either to collect larger sums of revenue through taxation or to borrow money. In 1930 for each 8 dollars of income workers paid 1 dollar in taxes. They paid a dollar for each 4 dollars of income in 1950. By 1992 they were paying a dollar in taxes for each three dollars earned. Now, they pay approximately 50% of their earned income in federal, state, and local taxes, and that figure is higher yet if one factors in all the hidden taxes. (Moore, 1993)

Unfortunately, that amount of taxes was not sufficient to pay for all the government's expenses. To cover the shortfall, which has occurred annually, with few exceptions since the beginning of FDR's administration, the government has borrowed money, both from its own citizens and from those of foreign countries. In 1993 the federal government was borrowing $700,000 million dollars a minute, $11,000 a second. That was going on every minute of every day. (Moore, 1993) And the amount of red ink in the budget has continued to grow. Federal revenue has increased as the government's monetary requirements have grown. In 1905 total direct revenue was $658 million. Within twenty years revenue was $4 billion. Within another 20 years it had grown to $53 billion, and in 1965, the year of the beginning of LBJ's Great Society programs, it was $116.8 billion. By 1985 it was $734 billion increasing to $2, 2162.7 billion in 2005. It had grown to $2,775.1 billion in 2013. (www.usgovernmentspending.com)

Federal spending has increased even faster than revenues as the various entitlement programs have expanded in number and scope. In 1960 total spending was $97.3 billion. Twenty years later the costs of the various Great Society entitlement programs increased expenditures to $590.9 billion. They rose to $1,789 billion in 2000 and to $3,457 billion in 2010. (www.usgovernmentspending.com) Obviously, a cursory examination of the data in the previous two paragraphs reveals that in spite of increasing revenue the politicians were spending even more than the government was collecting. The solution was to borrow the needed funds. In 1940 at the beginning of WWII the national debt was $42 billion. By 1960 it was $286 billion. As the government's expenses rose to pay for the entitlement programs, the national debt jumped to $907.7 billion in 1980. By the year 2000 it had increased to $5,674 billion. Still going up, it was $13,561.6 in 2010. Total federal debt passed $17,536 billion in 2014 with predictions that it was headed even higher. (www.treasurydirect.gov) In fact, there were dire predictions that at some point in the future entitlement costs might consume the entire federal budget.

Undoubtedly, the tremendous amount of money spent on entitlements was well meant, and it did indeed provide relief to millions of Americans through the years. Scores of people will swear that they could not have survived without assistance from the government. In the individual sense the programs were a force for assistance to the needy and the elderly.

However, in a larger sense overall effects may have been more negative than positive. The poverty rate has remained basically unchanged since the beginning of the war on poverty in spite of the fact that millions receive government entitlements monthly. Notwithstanding all our health care programs including Medicare and Medicaid the health care rating for the U. S. was 38th, although it was first in spending on health care. (en.wikipedia.org) Life expectancy in the U. S. was one year below the international average, ranking 26th just behind Slovenia. (In the 1970s prior to the full effect of the various entitlement programs life expectancy in the U. S. was number 1 in the world.) (Kliff) In a ranking of the 10 countries with the best retirement systems the U. S. was number 10.

(www.thinkadvisor.com) Most surprising of all, in a survey of the Index of Economic Freedom based on four criteria: 1. the rule of law, 2. limited government, 3. regulatory efficiency, and 4. open markets the U. S. ranked 12th just behind Estonia. (The U. S. rating was 75.5 while the number 1 ranked Hong Kong's rating was 90.1) (www.heritage.org)

What Are The Differences?

Rights are fundamentally different from entitlements. Rights are God-given; entitlements are government-given. Rights enable us to be independent; entitlements cause many of those receiving payments to become permanently dependent. Rights give us the freedom to be ourselves and to become what we have the ability and the desire to become; entitlements rob us of the need to provide for ourselves and to enjoy the resultant feelings of satisfaction. Rights minimize the intrusion of government in our lives; entitlements in the end maximize it. Rights give us the joy of filling our cup of life; entitlements lead to the assumption that the government has the responsibility of filling our cup for us. Rights enable us to become victors; entitlements eventually cause us to conceive of ourselves as victims. Rights make us responsible; entitlements cause us to shift our responsibility to others. Rights foment hope, progress and achievement; entitlements result in despair, stagnation and failure. Rights expect people to strive toward maximum achievement; entitlements encourage people to sink to embittered acceptance of minimum maintenance. Rights expect people to contribute to the creation of wealth; entitlements encourage people to consume wealth. Rights are objective and limited; entitlements are subjective and unlimited. Rights lead to "life, liberty, and the pursuit of happiness"; entitlements lead to existence, dependence, and the expectation of government solutions to individual problems. Rights limit government and liberate the individual; entitlements expand government and enchain the individual. Rights stimulate economic growth; entitlements curtail it by authorizing government to take from some in order to give to others. Rights promote equality; entitlements in the name of equality result in inequality. Rights are permanent; entitlements are constantly growing as wants based on subjective desires supported by advocacy groups and politicians pursuing their own agendas contribute to constantly rising expectations. Rights are based on freedom to be and to do; entitlements are based on egalitarianism, redistribution of wealth, and transfer payments. Rights provide incentives to creativity and production; entitlements act as disincentives to creativity and production. Rights are the result of a long evolutionary struggle to protect God-given freedoms from government encroachment; entitlements are the consequence of politicians' using other people's money to provide benefits in exchange for recipients' votes.

The following fictitious anecdote illustrates the difference between rights and entitlements.

Three men love turkey. They all want a turkey dinner for the holidays. John X has three prize turkeys in his back yard. He started with five planning to sell four to pay for his feast. However, two died shortly after he got them. He has been feeding the three remaining turkeys high-protein feed for months watching them get bigger and fatter every day. Just looking at his birds fills his mind with the image of a golden-brown turkey fresh from the oven and steaming on his table. His mouth waters at the thought. He can hardly wait.

John Y would also like a turkey dinner. The problem is that he has no turkey nor does he have any money to buy one. However, he has seen the turkeys that John X is feeding, and he thinks that one of those would be delicious.

He has a plan. One night about two in the morning he slips cautiously into John X's yard and quietly removes one of the turkeys from its pen. He leaves the scene with all possible haste.

John Z, too, would like to enjoy a turkey dinner, and he, also, has seen John X's turkeys. The difficulty is that he is in the same situation as John Y. He has no turkey and no money. However, he has a plan. He knows a government bureaucrat in charge of the local entitlement agency. He goes to the agency office and describes his plight. He really wants that turkey, and he feels that he is entitled to a turkey for the holidays. Having turkey on the holidays is an American tradition, and he is an American. His sympathetic listener agrees, goes to John X, takes one of the two remaining turkeys, returns to John Z, and gives him the turkey.

What are the similarities and the differences among the courses of action of the three men? John X exercises his right to the pursuit of his happiness and the possession of property. He assumes the responsibility of satisfying his desire while at the same time not interfering with the rights of anyone else. John Y also chooses to pursue his happiness, but in the process he violates the property rights of John X. He commits a crime, and, if he is caught, he will be punished. John Z, too, has a plan for satisfying his wants. However, he commits no crime. He enlists the aid of the government to take the turkey from John X in order to give it to him. He commits no crime because it is the government worker who takes the turkey from John X to give it to him because he is entitled to it.

What Are The Consequences?

The result in the case of the turkeys is quite logical. John X raises no more turkeys in the future. John Y, if he gets caught, vows not to get caught next time. John Z expects the government to continue supplying his turkey for the holidays.

Individually such incidents seem relatively insignificant for society as a whole. However, expanded into millions of cases yearly the effects are enormous. They permeate the entire economic system and the natural social structure. No one can avoid the all-pervading consequences. There is no escape for producers who must contribute a portion of their gain to support those who receive entitlements. Nor is there escape for recipients who are drawn gradually into an existence dependent upon regular transfusions of wealth from the producers of society through government agencies to non-producers in our society.

Unquestionably, the effect on all individuals is undesirable. Unable to keep the rewards of their initiative, ingenuity, and labor, many producers perceive the realities of the system and reduce their efforts thereby diminishing their achievement and their contribution to society. Kept by government payments, non-producers take advantage of the programs and fall into an almost irresistible dependency resentful of the system that maintains them in economic survival status but social and psychological despair. The result is that they make no contribution to the overall welfare of society.

The entitlement burden placed on individual members of society spreads throughout a nation diminishing overall production. Whenever some are not permitted to keep the goods produced by their labor and/or whenever others do not have to work to survive, significant repercussions ripple throughout society inevitably altering the forces that supply the energy and vigor necessary for a high quality standard of living. The multiple disincentives to production impose an inescapable and enervating liability on the economy that subsequently weakens society as a whole.

For example, a few years ago professors at a major Mid-Western university devised a program to teach inner-city, welfare children to work and to save money. Directors planned to obtain jobs for the teenagers and to teach them to save money from their salary. However, the negative response on the part of the youngsters and the fierce opposition on the part of their parents quickly put an end to the well-intentioned plans of the program directors. What fostered these unanticipated reactions? In the first place, the young people could not understand why they should get a job and work when their family received a check every month without doing anything. In the second place, the families were totally opposed to such a program because they were afraid that if the authorities found out about their children working they would reduce their child dependency payments.

While compassionate government bureaucrats and self-indulging politicians tend to produce permanent welfare dependents, responsible parents seek to teach their offspring to become self-reliant and independent. They realize that the best gift that they can give to their children is to bring them to a point at which they will not need their parents. Human parents work long and hard to instruct children in their moral values and to give them an education. Most wild-animal parents do the same. They provide guidance to their offspring in protecting themselves, obtaining food, and finding shelter. Even adult wild animals lose their incentive and ability to forage if they live in a location in which their food is provided all the time. Perhaps contemporary politicians could learn a valuable lesson from parents, both human and animal.

Government policies may have positive or negative effects. Protection of individual, God-given rights results in positive actions and reactions in society. Unchecked promotion of government-given entitlements leads to negative actions and reactions. Rights encourage producers to be the best that they can be. Entitlements lead to the proliferation of the number of non-producers in society because government payments reward dependency. The result is disillusionment at many levels of society. Producers resent having so much of their labor confiscated to give to someone who is not working while recipients feel themselves to be victims of the system. The resultant situation is that no one is satisfied and fewer and fewer people trust the government and support its policies. Gradually, society is weakened because like all intricate organisms society is the sum total of its individual components. Slowly but surely, the economy deteriorates because, like society, the economy is a product of the contributions of individual members of the whole. In the end, the government also becomes dysfunctional because government depends upon the active support, participation, and contribution of all the citizens. Like agriculture the society, the economy, and the government depend upon the implementation of a sustainable system for its present health and future existence. Debilitated by too many disincentives all three weaken, wilt, and wither away.

Unquestionably, a system of widespread entitlements is unsustainable. It is a matter of time until the load becomes too burdensome for the productive members of society to bear. Ever-growing numbers of entitlement dependents increase beyond the capability, and willingness, of the wealth producers to support them.[1] As Margaret Thatcher said, "Eventually, politicians run out of other people's money". When politicians are finally forced to reduce entitlement spending, recipients react angrily to having their accustomed financial support reduced, or even eliminated. If the situation is not handled prudently, it may deteriorate into demonstrations, riots, and even chaos, which creates an opportunity for self-serving opportunists to assume dictatorial control of the country.

Conclusion

Historically, the concept of rights has protected individuals from government oppression. In more recent times entitlement programs have provided government benefits, i. e., taxpayer-funded benefits, to non-producing members of particular groups in society. Rights are inviolate. Entitlements are not rights. A firm belief in rights ensures individual freedom and leads to self-reliant individuals, a strong society, a vigorous economy, and a limited government. A commitment to the maintenance of ever-increasing entitlement programs restricts individual freedom, sickens society, weakens the economy, and expands government.

---

[1] As one of my colleagues from England remarked, "We thought that if we gave them all those perks they would continue to work, but they didn't!"

Since governments have no funds of their own, the only way they can provide benefits to some is to violate the property rights of others. If the viewpoint that entitlements are rights becomes widespread, there will be no rights, because only by violating individual rights can governments obtain the funds to provide the promised benefits, and surely there can be no entitlements if there are no rights.

Americans who do not understand the difference between rights and entitlements and the consequences of each place at risk their future and that of their country. Unchecked dependence upon entitlement programs can result in an unbearable economic and social burden that overwhelms the decreasing number of producers in a vain effort to feed the swelling tide of non-producers.

Selected References

"A Rancide Slew of Legislation." Investor's Business Daily. 23 July 2014. apps.leg.wa.gov

Brown, Michael K. ed. Remaking the Welfare State: Retrenchment and Social Policy in America and Europe. Philadelphia: Temple University Press, 1988.

Budget of the United States Government Fiscal Year 1994. Washington, D. C.: U. S. Government Printing Office, 1993.

"Dodd-Frank: Four Years of Failure." Investor's Business Daily. 23 July 2014.

de Rugby, V. "How Many Workers Support One Social Security Retiree?" Mecatus Center, George Mason University. 22 May 2012.

"Ending Welfare As We Know It." Investor's Business Daily. 28 July 2014.

Ferrara, P. "America's Ever Expanding Welfare Empire." Forbes. 22 April 2011.

Gattuso, J. L. and S. Keen. "Red Tape Rising: Regulations in the Obama Era." www.heritage.org. 31 March 2010.

Georges, Christopher. "Clinton Now Faces a Race With GOP Congress To Cut Taxes, Budget While Protecting His Base." The Wall Street Journal 14 Nov. 1994.

"Is the Government Also Monitoring the CONTENT of Our Phone Calls?" WashingtonBlog. 6 June 2013.

Joffe-Walt, C. "Unfit for Work." Planet Money. apps.npr.org.

Kessler, G. "How many pages of regulations for Obamacare?" www.washingtonpost.com.

Kliff, S. "The U. S. Ranks 26th for life expectancy, right behind Slovenia." The Washington Post. 21 November 2013.

Moore, S. "The Growth of Government: 1980—2012." www.forbes.com. 24 January 2013.

Moore, S. "The Growth of Government in America." fee.org, 1 April 1993.

Muhlhausen, D. B. and P. Tyrrell. "The 2013 Index of Dependence on Government." www.heritage.org.

Murray, C. In Our Hands, A Plan to Replace America's Welfare State.

Olasky, Marvin. The Tragedy of American Compassion. Washington, D. C.: Regnery Gateway, 1992.

Poverty in the United States: 1991. Washington, D. C.: U. S. Government Printing Office, 1992.

Sauter, M. A., C. B. Stockdale, and D. A. McIntyre. The 10 countries where people save the most money." Fox Business. 15 August 2011.

Schlafly, P. "Microsoft Job CutsUnderscore Immigration-Reform Hypocrisy." Investor's Business Daily. 23 July 2014.

Segalman, Ralph and Asoke Basu. Poverty in America: The Welfare Dilemma. Westport, Connecticut: Greenwood Press, 1981.

Snyder, M. "The U. S. Government is Monitoring All Phone Calls, All Emails and All Internet Activity." InfoWars.com. 7 May 2013.

Spindler, Arthur. Public Welfare. New York: Human Services Press, 1979.

Statistical Abstract of the United States 1993. Washington, D. C.: U. S. Government Printing Office, 1993.

64

Thomas, Paulette. "Bipartisan Panel Outlines Evils of
Entitlements, But Hint of Benefit Cuts Spurs Stiff
Opposition." The Wall Street Journal 8 Aug. 1994.
Volgeli, W. Never Enough: America's Limitless
Welfare State. www.en.wikipedia.com
www.governmentspending.com
www.gpo.gov
www.heritage.org
www.taxfoundation.org.
www.thinkadvisor.com
www.usgovernmentrevenue.com
www.washingtonpost.com

The Income Tax: Real Reasons for Keeping the Present Income Tax System

Some of my friends don't believe a bit in the present income tax system. They would do away with it. In all honesty, they don't like keeping every piece of paper the whole year long, filling out those incomprehensible forms, giving the government nearly forty percent of what they make, and trying to convince the IRS that they are innocent when they accuse them of being guilty. They would do away with it all. They would try anything—a flat tax, a national sales tax, a value-added tax, the honor system, no tax, anything—just to get rid of that dreaded income tax.

Not me. There are real reasons for keeping the present income tax system.

1. The reason that I like best is that it soaks the rich. I admit it is a "pain in the you know what", but the rich have to pay more than I do. That's good. They should pay more than the rest of us. They have more than we do so they should have to pay more. I like that.

2. Another reason is that it creates lots and lots of jobs, millions probably. Think about it for a minute. Think of all those people who would lose their jobs if there were no income tax system in this county: the IRS employees, the tax lawyers, the accountants, the lobbyists, the employees of the paper companies (lost revenue from millions of pages of paper no longer needed), the employees of the drug companies (mainly those making aspirin and anti-depressions medicine), the employees of the companies making calculators, and, most important, the writers of the tax laws, not to mention the employees of companies that make file cabinets, folders, pens, pencils, and erasers. The suffering that I go through each year preparing for April 15th may not be the least bit pleasant, but I would not want on my conscience the hardships of the millions who would lose their jobs if the present income tax system was abolished.

3. It is responsible for a healthful and invigorating collective national sigh of relief every year on April 15. Thus, it serves as a marvelous catharsis as the termination of our annual period of pain and suffering. Prior to April 15 large numbers of common citizens undergo long periods of gloom and depression, but afterwards, a wonderful transformation occurs. Steps are lighter, smiles are broader, spirits are lifted. It's over! It's over for another year! That is a good feeling.

4. It also has another function generally overlooked except by those who benefit. It gives tax advantages to special groups. That's right. It's the law, and, if you have a special knowledge of the hundreds of pages of tax laws, or if you are rich enough to hire a smart tax lawyer, you can pick you way through the tax requirements without having to meet them all. All of you have to pay is what the law requires, and if you know the law well enough, you don't have to pay as much as the other people who don't know the law so well, or who are not rich enough to hire the lawyers to help them escape the snares of the tax laws.

5. It discourages earnings, savings, and investments. A tax is a penalty, and, if you want to discourage some type of entity or activity, you tax it. Sounds strange. However, that's true, and that is good. If the income tax system did not discourage taxpayers from earnings, savings, and investments, some people would have more than they really need. Of course, they do anyway, but with the income tax the government can keep that tendency to a minimum.

6. It supports a system in which the money goes to the government rather than to the people who work for it and earn it. Now, some of my friends don't believe it, but that is a good system. Otherwise, the people who produce the wealth to earn the money   would have it themselves to spend, which is bad because they might not spend it wisely like the government. They might spend it on their own selfish desires rather than on the common good identified by the politicians and government bureaucrats.

7. It surely forces taxpayer to keep records. I suspect that if the IRS did not insist, most of us would not have shoe boxes filled with receipts and canceled check scattered throughout the house. We do not do such

things by choice, and it is good that the government insists that we do what we should do without having to be made do it.

8. A corollary to the previous reason is that prevents us from wasting time participating in aimless and useless activities. At the same time it reaches us mental discipline by forcing us to devote a considerable portion of our time and energy to doing something that we find totally distasteful and objectionable.

9. It has an indirect positive effect on our psyche—it gives us a sense of satisfaction due to the painful compliance with the obligation of citizenship. Consciously, or subconsciously, we all feel a faint sense of martyrdom walking up the mail box, heaving a sigh of relief, and dropping in our tax returns.

10. It also keeps us on our toes. No one seems to be smart enough to understand and to remember all the various stipulations and exceptions to the tax laws, not to mention the Job-like patience required to plow through them in the first place. We have to be flexible in our uncertain attempts to meet the requirements, and we have to be prepared after filing to respond immediately to any unexpected correspondence from the IRS stating that their computers have detected some unspecified error in our return and that we have X number of days to correct the error.

11. Of course, their monstrous, ever-vigilant computers already know our earnings. We can keep no secrets. Their computers already know what our required income tax payment is, but sending us a bill for our taxes due would be no fun. The present system gives the IRS the opportunity to play the "I gotcha" game. Every time we make some unintentional error or overlook some income due to the amount of records that we have to keep or the complexity of the tax system they get to play with us, which must be a good thing because their unpleasant task must be inconceivably monotonous. They deserve some relief.

12. It fosters a definite sense of camaraderie among the tax payers. We all understand what the others are going through. We are all in the same boat. When we detect that annual pre-filing malaise settling on our friends and

co-workers, we can sympathize. We can feel their pain. It's good to realize that we are not alone. There are millions of others who feel just the same way.

13. It certainly promotes creativity. For the most part, taxpayers are not law breakers. However, their quest for ways and means either of avoiding or of deferring the payment of taxes never ceases. Of course, they are highly motivated in their search, and they become extremely adept at achieving their goal—to hand over the lowest possible percentage of their earnings to the government. I think that this is good and that it has a beneficial carryover effect on earners' abilities in their other pursuits as well. Think of the additional quantities of intellectual potential unleashed simply because their brain was stimulated and exercised to beat the income tax system.

14. One indisputable salutary effect of the present income tax system on the national psyche is the steady stream of jokes and cartoons making fun of the IRS. They add impressive amounts of jolly jogging to our daily routine. Without them we would have many fewer laughs during the year, and that surely would be lamentable.

15. Among many earners it perpetuates a strong sense of fatalism, uselessness, and powerlessness. "There are only two things you have to do in life—pay taxes and die." "I'll never get anywhere. The government takes so much that I don't have much left over for myself and my family." "There's nothing you can do. Just give them the money and keep quiet."

Ha. Ha. Ouch, it hurts. But, you know, perhaps, that is not such a bad way for us to feel. If we were too independent and sure of ourselves, we would probably be unmanageable and incorrigible, always causing trouble and demanding our rights.

16. It is a very efficient system for extracting duty from earners, especially those working for a salary. The company simply deducts the government's share and gives the remainder to the earner. This is a great system because the government never fails to get its share first. What is left over goes to the earner. Otherwise, the earner might not have it to give to the government when the scheduled payment date arrives.

17. It supplies huge quantities of money for the pet projects of politicians and bureaucrats. With all that money rolling into the nation's coffers the dispensers of Washington largess can fund projects for local communities that they would other wise be unable to afford. There are countless numbers of restored train stations, dams, airports, stadiums, etc., around the country that would not exist without funding from this gravy train.

18. The funds from the income tax provide financial support for our entire political system, and where would our country be without our political system and our politicians? Basically, politicians promise us all sorts of good things, things that are for those that they would like to serve, in order to "buy" our vote. These promises normally cost lots of money, money provided by the taxes on our income. With our money they get their colleagues to fund the promised projects, which pleases the voters and assure their vote in the next election thus promoting the political system and the politicians who control the system.

19. It provides a legal means of catching and sentencing big-time crooks. Those who operate in the shadowy world of illegal activities regularly escape the law with regard to their "business". However, IRS agents can indict them for failure to pay their income taxes. It is a good feeling to know that criminals are behind bars today because the income tax system provided a means for convicting them and putting them in jail.

20. It clearly helps support the U. S. Postal System. The weeks prior to and including April 15 must be one of their best periods of the year. Well, it probably does not equal the Christmas rush, but I would guess that the pieces of mail, and the profits, are among the highest of the year.

21. It helps the government. The politicians and bureaucrats need lots of money, and the income tax system is a good system for doing that. Of course, nothing can satisfy the unfettered gluttony of Washington. However, the system comes as close as any, and that provides us earners and taxpayers with a certain degree of satisfaction for having done our part to pay Uncle Sam's bills.

22. And finally, I am so impressed by the tax code itself—73,000 pages! (www.fairtax.org) Is that not

impressive? What an example of bureaucratic complexity! I can imagine those tax agents just sitting and looking at those tomes with pride and satisfaction. Pride and satisfaction in the first place because embedding such a large number of words in incomprehensible sentences is a feat to be feted for sure. Pride and satisfaction in the second place because having this impenetrable maze of rules and regulations to support any decision against unsophisticated taxpayers must build unwavering confidence in even the most timid agent. Gotcha! Gotcha!

A Better Way

All right! I confess! I was not serious! The income tax is a terrible tax! It is a negative factor on the economy, and it certainly hurts taxpayers. The fact that there have not been protests and uprisings against this illogical and detrimental system of collecting taxes is incomprehensible. Americans are remarkably docile and law-abiding people. Otherwise, they would have rebelled.

Even sadder than the system itself is the fact that the government could collect needed revenue without all the rules and regulations, without IRS enforcement, without all the accountants, without all the paper, without all the record keeping, and without all the painful hours spent trying to complete the latest tax forms.

That's why I am in favor of the Fair Tax.

The Fair Tax is a one-time tax on all goods and services for personal consumption.

There would be no federal income tax, no alternative minimum tax, no corporate income tax, no capital gains tax, no gift tax, and no estate tax.

There would be no need to keep records. (en.wikipedia.org)

There would be no Internal Revenue with its 85,000 employees.

There would be no social security tax, no Medicare tax, and no self-employment tax.

There would be no tax on used items.

There would be no double taxation.
(www.moneycrashers.com)

Just think about it! Just think about it!

Promises, Promises, Promises:
The Great Game of Politics

Introduction

"Yes, I promise to call before you leave." "Yes, I promise you." "Yes, you can count on it. That's a promise."

We may use the word, promise, in different ways. When we use it as a transitive verb, as in the first quote, it means that we are assuring the person addressed that we will do that which is stated after the verb. When we use it as an intransitive verb, as in the second quote, it means that we are making a pledge that will cause the person addressed to expect us to keep our word. When we use it as a noun, as in the third quote, it serves as a declaration that we will do whatever we say that we will.

Promises are pledges. When we make a promise, we are pledging that we will do just as we have said that we would. We make promises because we want people to believe us and to believe that we will keep our word.

Of course, promises made are not always promises kept. Sometimes, we really intend to keep our promises, but we forget, or we change our mind, or we are unable to keep them due to altered circumstances. At other times, we may never intend to keep our promises. In such instances we utilize promises as a deceptive but effective ploy in our strategy to convince others to believe that we will do as we say, even though we have no intention of complying. Operating on the subconscious, or conscious, tenet that the ends justify the means, we utilize promises as a tactic to sway other people in ways that will further our own desires.

What is the effect of promises? If they are kept, the effect is positive on those who remember. Based on past experience, we develop a trust in the word of those making the promises. Their promises are pledges to be kept, and we learn to believe that they will do as promised and to trust that they will keep their word. Of course, if we do not remember the promises, no positive or negative effects accrue. On the other hand, if they make promises and fail to keep their word, and, if we remember the promises and their subsequent failure to comply, the resultant effect is obviously negative. We will assume that we can not believe them, and, consequently, we will ignore their promises. We develop a sense of suspicion and cynicism toward those persons, and we are reluctant to take their promises seriously.

Politicians make promises. They make lots of promises. Data from various 2000 senatorial campaigns reflect this political tactic and attest to its effectiveness. In Michigan Stabenow proposed $672 billion dollars in spending increases to Abraham's $192 billion. In Minnesota Dayton proposed $2.28 trillion in spending increases to Grams' $130 billion. In New Jersey Corzine proposed $1.15 trillion in spending increases to Franks' $287 billion. In New York Clinton proposed $2.42 trillion in spending increases to Lazio's $3.87 billion. (Capital Ideas, Nov-Dec 2000)

Guess who won in each race??? Of course, all the candidates were quite generous in their proposals to increase spending of taxpayers' money. And why not? They have an office to win, and, if they win, the money that they will be spending is not theirs. Those voters who voted for them will even be grateful that the politicians they elected are spending their money to give them what they wanted, and that they themselves are paying for.

In fact, promises are a favorite means utilized by most candidates to energize their supporters and to bring others into their camp. They make them repeatedly believing, apparently with considerable justification, that with sufficient repetition all promises no matter how illogical they may be will take on an aura of authenticity. They either promise to continue present policies because they are popular with the electorate or to clean up the mess created by the incumbents because the current state of affairs is unpopular with potential voters. Citizens blamed Herbert Hoover for the Great Depression in the United States, so Franklin Roosevelt won the Presidency by promising them a "New

Deal". Lyndon Johnson sought to solve the many problems facing our country by creating the "Great Society". When that drive faltered under Jimmy Carter, Ronald Reagan became President by convincing the country that the federal government in Washington was the problem, not the solution. George Bush became President by promising to continue Ronald Reagan's supply-side economics. When the Reagan economic boom stuttered momentarily under the oversight of George Bush, Bill Clinton, conducting a campaign based on the motto, "It's the economy, Stupid.", told the American people that the economy at that time was the worst in the last fifty years and received more votes than either George Bush or Ross Perot in a three-way race.

What are voters to think? How are they to decide? Are politicians telling the truth? There is no possible way to know. If spoken truthfully, their promises do constitute a pledge. However, politicians may be unable to deliver on that pledge even if the intent and the desire are present. Of course, if spoken with no thought of implementation, promises amount to nothing more than a series of deceits utilized to increase the tally of their vote. In all cases promises are made in the present, but their implementation depends upon an uncertain and often unpredictable set of circumstances in an unforeseeable future.

Why then do politicians utilize promises as principal components of their campaign? Because they work. Voters seem to be eternal optimists. The supporters of each candidate want to believe, and they do. They believe, and they work, and they vote. In addition, their memories seem to be extremely short. When the next election occurs, they believe just as readily as they did in the previous election, and their emotions run just as high. What fun! Politics is a great game!

The Game Plan

Political campaigns are massive undertakings. They are tightly organized and carefully controlled efforts directed from a central office often referred to as the "war room".

The chain of command stretches from the campaign headquarters into the trenches of each and every precinct in the country. All potential voters and votes are sought assiduously and secured tightly. Their goal is "to get out the vote". As the old saying so graphically describes, "No stone is left unturned." The overriding and ever-present task of the campaign effort is to see to it that all voters are "turned" to their advantage. In essence, the staff, both paid and volunteer, conduct an intensive propaganda war to ensure that their candidate prevails in the morass of promises and counter promises, claims and counter claims put forth during the campaign.

Abraham Lincoln once said, "You can fool some of the people all the time; all of the people some of the time; but you cannot fool all the people all the time." Many, if not most, politicians seem to have adopted Mr. Lincoln's dictum. They have come to realize that they can indeed fool some of the people all the time, i. e., some groups vote for a particular party no matter who the candidates are, what they stand for, or what promises they make. They are also quite well aware that there are others in the electorate whom they can fool in any particular campaign. These voters may not always vote for any particular party, but they can be manipulated into voting for candidates making promises specific to their beliefs and desires. If they can line up enough of these single-issue voters to go with the voters who are "in the bag" for their party, they have an extremely good chance at winning the election.

Of course, the astute politicians in the great game of politics are fully aware that they can not fool all the people all the time. They understand that some voters are not susceptible to their promises. Those voters either remember broken promises from previous campaigns or comprehend that candidates make promises which they can not possibly fulfill. However, students of modern political campaigns understand that they do not have to fool these voters. In fact, they do not even have to give them serious attention. They know that in most national elections only slightly over fifty percent of the electorate take the time and interest to follow the campaign and to cast their ballot. (Actually, the number is most likely fewer than fifty percent due to the unknown number of illegal votes counted in that overall tally of votes cast. Apparently, there are a number of unscrupulous citizens who vote in a number of precincts or in more than one state. In addition, there are an unknown number of voters who sell their vote casting ballots at the direction of local political activists, and, furthermore, no one knows the number of deceased citizens for whom votes are cast in any given election.)

Therefore, they only have to convince and to energize slightly over fifteen percent of the voters in order to prevail in any typical political contest. In fact, the more people who disenfranchise themselves because of their disrespect for politicians and politics the fewer people politicians have to convince in order to win elections. Their desire is to get out the vote, but their strategy is to ensure that of the votes cast they receive enough votes to win the election. The smaller the percentage of people who vote the fewer people they have to move into their column.

How do the professional politicians and their strategists attract and hold the necessary fifteen plus percentage needed to win elections. First, they conduct polls. They start sampling early in the campaign, and they continue until the eve of the election. What does the public think? The results of these opinion samples become the basis for the propaganda campaign conducted on behalf of their candidate. When the trends become obvious, candidates quickly place themselves at the forefront and boldly declare themselves the "leaders" of the people's will. That is, in order to achieve their own personal ambitions, they pose as public servants. Second, they choose the promises that their candidates will make, the promises being based on the results of the polls that they have taken. Third, they attempt to convince the voters that they will give them more of what they want than will their opponent. Fourth, some politicians, not all, seek to create a class of citizens permanently dependent upon government support in order to ensure that they will always vote for care-giving government policies and care-giving politicians. Fifth, some politicians, not all, attempt to arouse group resentments against other groups by painting them as victims, victims whom they themselves recognize and whom they themselves are qualified to help. Sixth, all present-day politicians seek to portray themselves as being more sensitive to the plight of their constituents and more compassionate than is their opponent. Seventh, they never, ever tell the voters that the money needed to fund all these programs that they want and that will be so good for them will come out of their paycheck before they can get it. (In fact, the promising politicians are so adept at this ploy that many citizens are unaware that it is the taxpayers themselves who will actually pay for the benefits being promised. According to a Fox News poll (Investor's Business Daily, A 26, December 15, 2000), 50% percent of the polled sample believed that the government has money of its own to pay for the benefits it distributes, 11% were not sure, and only 39% understood that politicians must first confiscate the money from taxpayers in order to be able to fund their many promised programs.) Eighth, nor do they ever, ever tell them that providing them with these promises will require a vast bureaucracy and a practically incomprehensible array of regulations. The trick is to keep attention focused on the supposed benefits rather than the costs involved in implementing their promises, a feat at which they seem to be most adept, or perhaps, the fact is that we, the voters, are incredibly inept at recognizing their subterfuge.

Successful political leaders are remarkably skilled in manipulating the people for their own gain. One of the most ingenious in this regard was Santa Ana of Mexico. Early in his career while fighting the Americans at Vera Cruz, he lost a leg in battle. (Actually, he was wounded by a stray bullet while astride his horse well out of harm's way, which led to the amputation of the leg.) Later, he was clever enough to be at the head of his country's government a number of times. Once he even led a rebellion against his own regime! One reason he was so unusually successful in returning to power was that he always managed to survive being overthrown. When the victor in the power struggle considered dismissing his fallen opponent, Santa Ana would plead for clemency, mercy for a helpless fellow with only one leg! And the ploy worked! Repeatedly, his request was granted, and he left the field alive only to return again another day.

Characteristics of Skillful Politicians

We may not like politicians. In fact, we may dislike them intensely. We may not believe their promises. In fact, we may be convinced that they are plying us with false promises that they never intend to keep and that they are doing so just to be elected. We may not like the condescending way in which they treat us. In fact, we may resent the way they manipulate us in order to obtain our vote. However, we can not help admiring how well they do what they do. They are extremely skillful at raising money, at conducting campaigns, at creating a predetermined image, at developing a following, and at gaining, and holding, political power.

In the political battles called campaigns some politicians have a definite public-image advantage over their opponents. Those who make the best impressions are the following:

1. Those who are comfortable in crowds,
2. Those who are at ease in front of the TV camera,
3. Those who are agreeable to the news media opinion molders,
4. Those who are able to express their campaign themes in short sound bites for TV,
5. Those who are able to attract fervent followers,
6. Those who are able to say what people want to hear,
7. Those who are able to prevaricate with a straight face and without remorse,
8. Those who are unwavering in their commitment to their own cause, i. e., their election and the enactment of their views,
9. Those who have a pleasant voice and face

Clearly, some candidates have the ability to project a carefully-planned image more effectively that do other candidates. Voters respond positively to them and give them their support in the campaign and their vote in the election.

However, sooner or later a question inevitably arises. Are the characteristics of an effective campaigner the same as those of an effective leader? No, they are not, nor can they be because the job requirements are different. Of course, politicians who are able to project a likable personality and who are skillful communicators have the potential to become effective leaders because of their ability to gain the people's trust and to convince them of the correctness of the actions that they take, but their personality, their communication skills, and their rapport with the people do not make them effective leaders. Throughout the ages historians have recorded countless charlatans who have attracted legions of followers, lemmings who have run blindly after their leader convinced that they were doing the right thing. Political charm may be a curse as often as a blessing.

Effective leaders need charisma, but they also need much more. They also need to be able to organize a smoothly functioning government to administer the area over which they have jurisdiction. They need to be able to work with the other branches of government. They need to have a vision for programs that will be beneficial to our republic. They need to be prepared to work hard and to lead the people and members of other political persuasions into their view of the future, i. e., to build consensus. They need to be able to attract loyal aides and to distribute responsibility. They need to be flexible enough to consider alternatives and to make adjustments when events fail to develop as they had expected. They need to have a broad knowledge of government and how it functions. They need to plan for the long term realizing that they serve for the short term. They need to be honest. They need to have a stable character. They need to be and remain humble. They need to be able to learn not to take themselves too seriously. They need to keep constantly in the mind that their role is to serve the people, not themselves or their political party.

Political parties want to win elections in order to maintain or to gain power. In order to do so, they normally select their most effective campaigners to represent their party during election campaigns. Therefore, voters face a dilemma. Their republican responsibility is to choose an effective leader. Their choices consist of the most attractive campaigners that the political parties have to place in nomination. That is, the choice they are offered does not coincide with the choice that they need to make. In addition, their choice is made even more complicated by thirty-second sound bites, staged photo ops, and controlled TV debates plus selective and slanted media coverage.

Who has the advantages and who has the disadvantages? The advantages clearly lie with the political parties and their professional politician campaigners. Equally obvious is that the disadvantages lie with potentially effective leaders who are not the most effective campaigners and the voters who need to choose the best leader.

What Do Politicians Tell Us?

What do politicians tell us?

They tell us many things, of course, and we could delineate more than present space limitations permit. Those mentioned here are obviously selective. However, the important idea to remember is the principle: politicians tell us what is good for us in many areas of our life.

First, they tell us that social security is a great benefit. After we retire or if we become disabled, they will send us a check each month for the rest of our life. In addition, they will pay burial expenses of $256.00 when we die. (There is one caveat to the "death benefit". That is that only the first spouse to die receives burial expenses of $256.00. The second receives nothing. There must be some logic to that policy. However, I have been unable to determine what it might be.) They normally pass over the requirement that they must take out a portion of our paycheck each month before we receive it, or that as the number of retired persons increases and the percentage of workers to retirees decreases, there will not be enough money to fund this "pay-as-you-go" program.

Politicians are astute enough not to mention that the average social security payment to working men and women is currently around $1,000.00 per month while some serving in Congress will receive in their lifetime after leaving office a million dollars or more. With regard to the Vice Presidency and Presidency, former Vice President, Al Gore's pension begins at $94,800.00 per year, a potential lifetime pension of $5.96 million dollars. Former President Clinton could receive $7.29 million dollars if he lives to the end of his life expectancy. Nor do they dwell on the fact that it is the working people who fund their own monthly payments as well as those of the Vice President and President. For example, former Vice President Al Gore insisted that the present Social Security system should remain unchanged and intact. However, after defeat, even though he will receive close to one hundred thousand dollars per year for the remainder of his life, an aide stated in response to a question about Mr. Gore's future that he planned to "make some money" after being in the government for all his life!   Apparently, he himself would not be satisfied with the more normal $1,000.00 per month which he thought perfectly fine for the average voter.

Second, they tell us that Medicare is essential for us. Otherwise, we would not be able to take care of our health-care needs. They automatically enroll us in Medicare Plan A when we reach the age of sixty-five giving us the option of enrolling in Plan B. They normally do not stress the fact that Medicare does not actually pay for our medical needs. In fact, most retirees immediately purchase a Medicare supplement to pay for those aspects of their care not covered by Medicare. In addition, they simply do not acknowledge that the bureaucracy needed to administer the program and the resultant regulations have added to the paper work associated with health care thus driving up costs at a tremendous rate and unnecessarily complicating the work of doctors and nurses throughout the land.

Third, they tell us that we should support public education and that our children should attend public schools. They sometimes admit that discipline and academic achievement in the public schools are not the best, but they assure us that with more money they can solve these and any other problems. They do not mention the fact that parents who want their children to have a Christian education must either send them to private schools or educate them at home.

In addition, their laws require that parents with school-aged children pay taxes to support public education even though their children do not attend public schools. Of course, it is also true that many politicians urging us to support public education and to send our children to public schools enroll their own children in exclusive private schools.

Fourth, they tell us that we should pay higher taxes because they need the money to fund all their programs and, in effect, because they know better how to spend our money than we do. That is, their programs are more important than our own personal needs even though we are the ones who work and invest to make the money. They feel that the money is theirs rather than ours. Rarely, do they attempt to deal with the commonly-accepted fact of government waste, and even less often do they seek to streamline programs thereby lowering the cost of government. No mention is made of how easy it is to spend someone else's money to further personal political aspirations.

Fifth, they tell us that the people demand what they are doing. They have no choice really. They are only doing the will of the people. They do not focus attention on the funds and bureaucracy needed to provide those programs that we are told that we desire so strongly.

Sixth, they seek to convince us that they are our servants. They belong to us, and they will devote all their time and energy to providing those government services that we demand. They conveniently never mention the fact that they themselves potentially can become famous, powerful, and rich in the process.

Seventh, they believe that the rich should pay most of the taxes and that the collected funds should be redistributed among those who are not so rich, i. e., the lower and middle classes. Of course, the rich would automatically pay more taxes anyway because they earn more money. However, the politicians believe that should also pay a higher percentage of their income, which leads to a situation in which a minority, the rich, pay a major portion of the income taxes in this country.

Thus, those earning up to $10,000.00 pay 4% of

their income in federal income taxes. Those earning more than $500,000.00 pay 29%. The average dollar amount is $253.00 for the lowest income group and $847,000.00 for the highest income group. The average for all taxpayers is $7,824.00. Seventy percent of tax filers pay less than the average amount. Those with income in the top 7.5% pay 55% of the taxes. (Dollars & Sense, Nov-Dec 2000)

Of course, they do not address this situation. Theoretically, one person can pay $100,000.00 in taxes at a rate of 39% while another pays minimal taxes at an extremely low rate.

Eighth, they outline a situation in which the rich do not deserve the money that they are making because the only way to make money is to take it away from someone else, normally someone who is less rich. Therefore, a tax system in which money is taken from the rich and given to the poor is justified. It is simply a system of redistribution that serves as a system of retribution for the deplorable state of the victims of our economic system.

Ninth, they hold firmly to the capital gains tax because they do not want the rich to make so much money. They do not seem to be aware of the fact that rich people are the ones who invest their money to promote economic expansion to provide work and income for the supposed victims of the system. They never seem to acknowledge the economic need for positive incentives to foment investment as a means to expanding production thereby providing a potentially higher standard of living for everyone in our society.

Tenth, they strive to convince us that rich people should pay estate taxes. The fact that they have already paid taxes on their earnings prior to acquiring their estate is irrelevant. Rich people have more than the embedded political bureaucracy deems necessary. Therefore, they initiated and maintain a tax that removes part of the remaining estate when the rich die.

What Do Politicians Do?

What politicians do? That is, what do they do in relation to what they tell us to do?

First, they do not rely on social security benefits for their retirement. Social security may be good for us, but it is not sufficient for them. They need more than the social security system provides. They have their own retirement system, one with much more generous benefits. In addition, most politicians have access to other more lucrative revenues of income after retirement. They have the connections to earn a considerable income by serving on corporate boards, by serving as consultants to various companies who do business with government agencies, by giving speeches, and by writing books. For example, the mentioned speaking fee for former Vice President Al Gore was $80,000.00. Former first lady Hillary Clinton signed a book contract for $8,000,000.00.

Some sample yearly retirement benefits for former members of Congress are as follows: Hubbard, $53,908.00 (jailed); Vander Jagt, $84,049.00 (joined law firm); Rostenkowski, $108,614.00 (jailed); Sundquist, $45, 690.00 (governor of Tennessee); Bradley, $53,790.00 (presidential nominee); Hatfield, $102,162.00 (joined law firm); and Schroeder, $79,342.00 (joined trade association). (Capital Ideas, Nov-Dec 2000)

Second, they do not depend upon Medicare for their medical care. Their bills are paid. Having their health care limited to a system that provides for only partial coverage would not be fitting for someone of their status. In addition, most have sufficient funds to pay for their own medical bills even if they did not have Medicare.

Third, in general, they do not abandon their own children to the public schools. They have the knowledge and the means to send them to selective private schools where they will receive a solid academic preparation and meet the right type of people.

Fourth, they tell us that our money belongs to them. In spite of what they say the money does not actually belong to them. It belongs to us, the ones who created the wealth.

However, they do have a need for it, and they have a tremendous asset in their political ambitions if they can convince us that the money indeed is theirs rather than ours.

Obviously, they have a place to put all the money that they can collect because the more that that receive the more that they can promise to a new or existing constituency in order to attract their vote and to keep it in future elections.

There is no practical limit to their ability to spend any money that they can collect. Fifth, they justify their programs and their expenditures by stating that the American people want these programs and that they are willing to pay for them, which is true in some cases such as national parks.

In many cases, however, some of the people want the program because they receive some type of funding or service for free while others do not favor it because they pay for it without receiving any benefit. For this reason, many tax payers do not think kindly of freeloaders who depend unnecessarily on welfare support, although they are indeed willing to provide help to the truly needy who are incapable of helping themselves.

Sixth, they may paint a picture of a public servant whose only interest is to carry out the people's will. However, time after time politicians' actions reveal other less noble motives. Many are more intent on pushing their own programs, their own constituents, and their own party and lining their own nest than on promoting the welfare of the general public.

Seventh, they take advantage of the ever-present loopholes to avoid the very laws that they and their colleagues institute. They establish and oversee an unreasonably complex tax system that permits them, and other people with the means to hire tax lawyers, to escape many of the burdens placed on the backs of the predominant middle class taxpayers. Because they know how to take advantage of the system, they limit their taxes to the minimum while at the same time supporting a system dedicated to collecting the maximum from each of the less sophisticated tax payers.

Eighth, they have lawyer friends who owe them favors and who help them avoid capital gains taxes.

Ninth, their lawyer friends also help them avoid estate taxes.

Results

Most games end. They have results. There are winners and losers. The political game never ends. It goes on and on, at different times with different politicians to be sure, but it never ends. There are always politicians, and they continue to make promises to convince voters to vote for them.

What are the results? Are there winners and losers?

Of course, there are results in the great game of politics, and there are winners and losers. Not only do the candidates and their party win and lose the people also win and lose. What are the consequences?

Subtly, gradually, almost imperceptibly, rule by the people for the common good is replaced by rule by vested interest groups for their own purposes. The people have the mass but no power. The special interests have the clout and the connections to control political votes in their favor. The people fund the system with their taxes, but the special interest groups direct its focus and influence its use.

Subtly, gradually, almost imperceptibly the number of bureaucratic rules and regulations proliferate. Each new program requires another set of guidelines for controlling how the funds are to be administered, and each old program requires additional rules and regulations to close the loopholes and inconsistencies uncovered by subsequent problems in administration.

As identified recipients scramble for the available government largess, they divide into competing groups one against the other. Our group versus your group. Ours versus yours. The members of each group stress their unique needs and identity over that of other groups who also wish to have their share. Inevitably, a Balkanization of society occurs.

As individuals and groups turn to government agencies and programs to meet their needs, government responsibility for their welfare gradually replaces the traditional reliance on individual responsibility. The impression is given, promulgated by willing politicians intent upon achieving their political ambitions and maintaining their political power, that only the government has the funds and the resources, and often the compassion, to meet their needs.

Traditionally, in America's free enterprise system individual entrepreneurs identified among the members of our society a need and developed a product or a service to meet that need. As politicians have expanded their vision for the good of our society and multiplied the number of their promises, they have sought to initiate government agencies to meet those needs instead of waiting for the natural evolution of a free economy to occur. As the more powerful government expands, the less powerful private enterprise recedes.

As politicians devote greater and greater attention to all aspects of our society, they note conditions which they do not favor and those which they do seek to change and to control. The result is that they gradually begin to impose selected government regulations over certain components of our free enterprise system. Although control is not total, the effect ripples throughout the economy placing a restraint on the entire economic system.

Politicians run the government, and by law, which the politicians have enacted, the government makes the laws of the land. The right to make the laws also gives the politicians the right to control the expenditure of funds collected by means of tax laws.

The resultant concentration of law-making and money in capitals around the world means the concentration of power also, and any power begets more power. Bureaucracy grows and grows. Rules and regulations proliferate. Power increases. And the cycle begins again.

An ever-growing and recycling, complex system develops that is self-serving and self-perpetuating.

Once established, governmental agencies take on a phenomenal degree of immortality. The affected bureaucrats who run them can always justify their existence, and they always seem to be able to justify year by year an increase in the budget. The original cause for their creation may even disappear completely, but the bureaucrats toil on safe in the almost certain knowledge that their budget request will be granted and that they will be funded for yet another year.

Rules and regulations proliferate. Some indeed are necessary and useful; others are unnecessary and disruptive. Some are logical; others are illogical and ridiculous. Some are known; others are unknown. Some are obeyed; others are disobeyed. Of course, we should cede the right-of-way to emergency vehicles with a flashing red light and a siren. We understand that someone's life may be at stake. However, others seem less reasonable. For example, in one state a home owner can not be sued if the snow in front of the house has not been disturbed and someone receives an injury in a fall. However, the injured person can sue if the home owner has shoveled the side walk. The lamentable point is that there are so many rules and regulations that they fill thousands of pages making it impossible for most citizens to be aware of most of them.

The guiding principle of doing what is best for the country as a whole is lost in the clamor of vested interest groups requesting favors for themselves. Because organized groups exert the most pressure on them, politicians tend to concentrate on satisfying their demands. Thus, the needs of the general public, society in general, or the economy as a whole suffer from a lack of attention and a vision for the future.

The unspoken operating principle among politicians is maintaining power. Once elected, the campaign for the next election begins. They make generous use of the franking privilege to stay in touch with their constituents and to make sure that they are informed regarding how much their representative is doing for them and for their state. Not surprisingly, in public opinion surveys citizens invariably hold their own representatives in high regard even though they may have very little respect for politicians in general. Also, not surprisingly, is the extremely high re-election rate in the United States—approximately 98% in normal elections. Defeating an incumbent with all the advantages associated with holding political office requires a minor miracle.

Politics seem to foster a focus on short-term solutions rather than long-term policy. Politicians may have the best of intentions. However, their survival instincts warn them that re-election depends upon present actualities rather than future possibilities. Working to reform and to preserve social security for retirees may be a worthy cause. However, being able to announce a grant of federal funds for the construction of a local bypass permits the representative to make a public announcement, which results in widespread publicity and generates a reservoir of good will among the voters.

Politicians also are well aware that their path to personal power lies within their party. Therefore, they often give primary allegiance to party as opposed to their country. As much as we might prefer otherwise, we see evidences of this fact every day in the announcements made and the votes taken. If one party proposes a solution to a problem, the other opposes it, and vice versa. Progress slows to a crawl as the politicians and their party jockey for political advantage. They prosper, and the country suffers.

As a result of their frustration with the politicians, their constant string of broken promises, and their incessant wrangling, our country is now unfortunately populated with a large percentage of disillusioned voters who never vote, i. e., self-disenfranchised voters. Barely half now vote in national elections, and many of them do so out of loyalty to their country and to the democratic process rather than out of any expectation that the present situation will improve. Have politicians held them in too low esteem? Have they made, and broken, too many promises? Have they lost their confidence?

Conclusion

Political parties desire power in order to control the government in ways that they deem desirable. Politicians seek office within those political parties to further their party's goals and to further their own personal ambitions. To gain the office in which the power resides, they must conduct campaigns. During those campaigns they make promises, promises which they assume will strike a responsive chord with the voters. Often these promises entail the expenditure of public funds supplied by the taxpayers. The promises of benefits that will be forthcoming if elected are loudly proclaimed and repeatedly enunciated. However, the necessity of extracting the money from the purse of the taxpayers to pay for those programs is kept deceptively out of the discussion.

In fact, the politicians are so clever that they have even begun surreptitiously to pay for their own campaigns for political office with taxpayer funds. Of the $700 million dollars spent in the 2000 presidential election taxpayers paid nearly half, including a large portion of the costs of both the Democratic and Republican conventions--$46.5 million for the Republican, 71% of the total cost, and $53 million for the Democratic, 93% of the total cost. Of the money spent by the two principal candidates, George W. Bush and Al Gore 37% of the money raised by George W. Bush was from public funds while 62% of Al Gore's money was from the taxpayers.

Some voters are completely unaware that they must pay for those programs that they consider to be so indispensable. The politicians have been so clever that these voters, 50% in one survey, actually believe that the government can magically create the money to pay for these benefits, i. e., that in the case of the government there actually   is a "free lunch".

Politics is indeed a great game. The rules are simple, too. Make promises to give the voters something that they want. Don't tell them that you will pay for it with their money. Get elected. Enjoy fame, power, and prosperity.

Joe's Minority: How Free Can They Be?

During the discussion of <u>The Federalist</u> at our Great Books monthly meeting Joe complained, "I don't want the government taking care of me. I just want to take care of myself."

Assuming that present-day governmental policies represent what the American people want, we can reasonably conclude that most favor a compassionate "Big Daddy" government that will solve all their problems for them. At least they tend to vote for politicians who promise and promote that type of government. Those like Joe who wish to take care of themselves presently constitute a minority in our country. At least most successful politicians do not advocate budget restraint and a minor role for government in our society.

Well, those in the majority may reply, "Let Joe, and others who share his philosophy, take care of themselves. They can do whatever they like as long as they do not interfere with our rights. We want all those government programs, every one of them, and we will fight to keep them."

At first glance that practical philosophy sounds like a workable solution. Both the majority and the minority are seemingly able to pursue an approach to life that fits their philosophy. However, such is not the case. The political and economic reality is that promising politicians can permit freedom to those who believe in limited government and individual liberty only to a certain degree. "Big Daddy" has an enormous purse. He has huge expenditures, and he must regularly replenish his resources, which he does by extracting a portion of each person's labor and investments, to enable him to make good on at least some of the politician's promises.

Freedom Day, the day of the year which marks the end of the time that we must work for the government to pay our taxes, now occurs some time the latter part of May, which means that, on the average, we all work for "Big Daddy" for over a third of the year. (I have read that the serfs during the Feudal Period were required to give thirty percent of their produce to the feudal lord for his beneficence. Many of us contribute a larger percentage than that. However, we do have the right to vote, and we may choose to pursue interests other than making money, which shields us to some extent from the necessity of making the required annual contributions to "Big Daddy".)

Therefore, Joe and others sharing his philosophy may want to take care of themselves. However, they must first work the first five months of each year, almost, for "Big Daddy". "Big Daddy" gets his share first. After that, their earnings for the remainder of the year are theirs. (Of course, if one recognizes that consumers, the taxpayers, also pay the hidden taxes incorporated into the price of services they utilize and products they purchase, Freedom Day occurs at an even later date in the year.)

In addition, what "Big Daddy" supports he also typically wants to control. This aspect of the government is run by "Big Daddy's" Siamese twin, "Big Brother". "Big Brother" consists of the politicians and millions of bureaucrats who fill office spaces around the country formulating rules to care for us, even those like Joe who wish to care for themselves. The only criterion seems to be the following: Is the rule good for us, in the opinion of those who formulate the rules, or is it advocated by some influential vested interest group lobbying for the benefit of its partisans? Input from the citizens is minimal, and opportunities to make changes in adopted rules are rare if not non-existent. As former President Reagan so aptly described the philosophy of the proponents of big government, "If it moves, tax it. If it continues to move, regulate it. If it stops moving, subsidize it."

These regulations may be positive or negative. They may require that we do something or that we not do something. For example, all of us have seen signs in rest rooms in recent years telling us that we must wash our hands after using the facilities in the rest room. In fact, the responsible bureaucrats go beyond telling us to wash our hands. They tell us to use soap and how long to wash. Now, I am not opposed to washing hands. In fact, I do so regularly—sometimes even when I have not been to the bathroom and when I am not heading to the table to eat. However, as we all are fully aware, it is simply not true that we must wash our hands when using a public rest room. There is no one watching us, and we can do as we please, which may lead to a snicker and to marching triumphantly out of the restroom without washing one's hands. The results of ridiculed and ignored rules are negative even though the purpose of the rule and the rule itself are positive.

Reactions to this and other similar regulations are likely to be mixed. Some will obediently wash their hands as they are instructed. Others will resent this intrusion into their personal realm of responsibility and wash less often than they might otherwise have done. The rise in the number of teens who smoke may well be an example of the latter reaction, although the reasons for their smoking obviously varies from one to another.

Negative rules are also abundant. Signs such as "Don't walk on the grass." "No admittance." "No spitting." (A common regulation on signs in Spain.) "No loitering." are common. Of course, we should learn not to do many things, especially when in public or on public property. However, psychologists tell us that negative commands generally generate the opposite impulse in many of us. "Don't open this door." is easily understood, and it means what it says. It may, however, arouse an almost irresistible curiosity to investigate what is behind the forbidden door. We might well ask ourselves if the national lack of respect for authority and the general tendency to disobey regulations reflects an unconscious desire to express our personal independence without bureaucratic interference.

Rules and regulations may be direct or indirect. They may deal directly with us as individuals. For example, most state law requires that we buckle our seat belt while we are in a moving vehicle. Or the rule may require that we contribute X number of hours to community service, as is the case for some high school students in Maryland. Or the rule may require that we wear a helmet while riding a motorcycle.

As might be expected, many people resent and resist those laws enacted to protect them from themselves. In addition, some self-protection laws are practically impossible to enforce. For understandable reasons we all rebel against being burdened with laws that attempt to tell us how to take care of ourselves. My initial reaction during a visit to the former Communist-dominated Yugoslavia was one of surprise upon seeing my hostess pulling the seat belt across her lap without securing it in the holder on the other side. "Why don't you fasten your seat belt?" I inquired. "Simple," she replied with a fierce pride and grim determination. "They can make us do many things, but they can not make us buckle our seat belts!"

On the other hand, numerous rules are general regulations that affect everyone. Such rules touch us personally, but they are not rules directed at individuals per se. For example, government regulators have decided that certain additives must be mixed into our gasoline. Refiners must include them if they want to sell gasoline in this country. The rule is not directed toward individuals, but, indirectly, we are affected by it.

The additives are factors in the quality of the air we breathe and in the manner in which our car performs. On the one hand, they lower pollution. On the other, they make some people sick. However, whether or not they make some of us sick, their use is mandated by the laws of the land, and we have no choice of alternative types of gasoline. Individual needs are rarely recognized by "Big Brother's" minions, and those with individual needs are even less likely to receive any type of concession.

Another indirect regulation is the requirement that new cars come equipped with air bags. Somewhere, some time, some influential governmental group of regulators made the decision that having air bags on cars was a good idea. The resultant regulations soon became the law of the land, and all auto manufacturers must install them in order to sell cars in the United States. For many the result has been life saving; for others it has been life ending. Some are living because the air bag absorbed the force of the car colliding with another object. Others are dead because the deployed air bag covered their face suffocating them in their seat where they were held fast by their seat belt. Still, air bags are required by law for everyone, even those who might prefer not to have them in their car.

Another example of a general regulation that affects us all is the complex array of rules related to Social Security. They are all pervading and inflexible. Our individual situation and/or preferences are not considered. We can draw Social Security when the rules permit, not when we might otherwise choose. We must participate. We do not have the option of not joining or of resigning even though the return on the money that we make might be significantly greater in a different type of retirement program. Young people, for example, must send a rather sizable portion of their earned income to Washington for the Social Security Fund even though they may never get all their money back, or even any of it if the "pay-as-you-go" system collapses. After all, in the convoluted logic of those who make the laws our money is not ours until "Big Daddy" says that we can have it. Of course, it may not be there when we reach retirement age, but "Big Daddy" insists on directing the system for everyone as he dictates. As long as he can say that the system is solvent for another ten to twenty years, he is satisfied.

Indirect regulations are less obvious than the direct ones, but the intention to control our actions is the same. A revealing statement by a spokesperson for the CDC is a typical example. Statistics indicate that the number of STDs is on the rise. The concerned bureaucrats concluded that the cause is that too many young girls are drinking too much beer, which leads to increased incidents of sexual intercourse. Therefore, they proposed raising the tax on a bottle of beer by X percent, which would reduce the amount of drinking by teenage girls by X amount, which would lower the number of sexual contacts by X number, which would lower the cases of STDs by X number. If only solutions to our social ills were only so simple. If they were, "Big Daddy" could indeed solve all our problems, and undoubtedly he would welcome the opportunity.

Of course, one might venture to question their assumptions. How do they determine that raising the tax on a bottle of beer by X percent will have the imagined beneficial effects? Those of us outside the bureaucratic environment would probably have less confidence in their conclusions than they seem to have. No matter. If they can convince enough politicians, the taxes on a bottle of beer will be raised by law, and it will most likely remain at that level until some new crisis causes them to raise the tax more to eliminate another societal flaw that they have detected. Examination after the fact of the efficacy of most rules and regulations is not a frequently instituted quality control safeguard. Regulations are piled upon rules regardless of their effectiveness and their cost.

If doing so suits his purposes, "Big Brother" can even redefine what X means in our society. For example, many people probably believe that receiving a high school diploma means that graduates can read and do mathematics at the twelfth grade level. Not necessarily so. In some states "Big Brother" has established more practical criteria. In one state, for example, students must demonstrate on a test their ability to read at the sixth grade level and do sixth grade mathematics in order to graduate from high school. Of course, nationwide almost a third of our high school graduates are functionally illiterate. Nevertheless, the powers-that-be qualify them as high school graduates and award them a diploma.

No aspect of our society is beyond the reach of "Big Brother". If "Big Brother" decides that we should not have guns, pressure to eliminate that privilege is applied. If "Big Brother" sanctions abortion and euthanasia, as is now the case in Oregon, is it conceivable that he might in some future economic or social malaise permit or even mandate the elimination of the unproductive? If "Big Brother" wants some part of a farmer's land, he condemns it and takes it. If "Big Brother" believes that tobacco smoke is harmful to our health, he raises the taxes on each package thereby raising the price, restricts advertising, and prohibits minors from buying tobacco products. (I might add that in this particular case my preferences correlate comfortably with the regulations.

However, I must ask myself why the same criteria are not applied to the sale and use of alcoholic beverages. The only answer that seems plausible to me is that those who make our laws must favor drinking more than smoking. Certainly both have far reaching detrimental outcomes in our society. Nonetheless, one might also argue that my personal decision not to smoke or to drink alcoholic beverages does not give me the right to deny others the right to make their own decision regarding those two practices.)

Returning to The Federalist--the authors were clearly concerned about the need to protect citizens from the ever-present threat of "factions" to dominate and control others in our body politic, which was one of the motives for establishing a government characterized by "checks and balances".

Among the questions that now confront us in the United States, and in other welfare states as well, are the following: Can a group that purports to have our best interests in mind become a faction? Have the politicians, the bureaucrats, and the members of the special interest groups that seek to influence them become factions in present-day America? If so, did the authors of The Federalist anticipate such factions? If so, what was their recommendation for protecting us, both the majority and the minority, from them?

Helping the Poor:

Guilty or not Guilty?

Our small group of friends has just completed a bountiful and delicious dinner. Stuffed and satisfied, we are leaning back in our chairs cheerfully commending our hosts for the fine meal.

Gracious as ever, our hostess acknowledges our gratitude, but in a moment of seriousness reflecting her compassionate nature she turns our attention elsewhere, "You know. We have so much while others have so little. We should help them. I feel guilty about not helping more, don't you?"

"No. I do not feel guilty. I don't feel guilty in the least." the accountant among us replies.

Slightly disturbed by such a conviction, the hostess questions his attitude. "How can you not feel guilty? Do you not have to admit that all of us around this room have more than we need to live and enjoy good health? Furthermore, do you not have to admit that many poor people are barely able to survive?"

The accountant nods his head in agreement. "Certainly, we are most richly blessed. We do have more than we need, more than we deserve, even more than is good for us. Equally true is the obvious fact that many unfortunate individuals struggle for the bare necessities of life."

Thinking that she is at the point of implanting just a tiny seed of guilt into this seemingly uncaring manipulator of figures, she pushes her apparent advantage, "Then should we not be more than willing to share from our excess with those in deprivation?"

"I sincerely doubt, and surely hope, that no one here would refuse assistance to someone truly in need, and I trust that the same can be said of all other members of our society who have managed to conserve or to create wealth more than sufficient to meet their own needs. However, accepting the existence of such universal human kindness does not eliminate or even alleviate poverty. The existence of compassion feeds no one. Acts of compassion feed the hungry, but feeding the hungry may do little or nothing to elevate the living standards of the poor."

Jack, who has been listening quietly, joins the conversation, "Come on, John. Marge is talking about helping those who are in need. She is not talking about a philosophy of beneficence toward the poor nor about governmental assistance programs."

"I realize that. However, poverty and its cures are much more complex than simply giving food, housing, health care, and legal assistance to those who are unable to afford it on their own. What we all want is to devise a system that will result in a better life for those now living in poverty. The question is how to accomplish that noble and humanitarian objective while maintaining the drive and vigor of all other segments of society. In addition, we must be careful not to degrade those helped in such a way as to destroy their self-respect, their self-will, and their motivation to become independent, productive members of society."

"Well, I brought up governmental assistance programs, and I think that they are a good idea. The government must have dozens, perhaps even hundreds, of programs to help those with incomes below the established poverty level. And charities. Think of all the charities and church organizations who provide assistance to the poor."

"Good point. That is the approach that we have taken in the past. Unfortunately, this traditional method of giving to the poor has done little to relieve poverty. In fact, the percentage of our population living below the poverty level has changed very little since the inauguration of President Johnson's War on Poverty."

At this point Marge asks an accusing question, "Are you implying that we should not try to help the poor?"

"No, of course not."

"Well, what do you think we should do?"

"I don't know. No one has all the answers. However, some of the questions that we should ask are obvious. First, how do we determine who needs help and who does not? That is, how do we distinguish between those who are unable to support themselves and those who can do so but prefer to have someone else provide their support?

Second, how should we help those unable to help themselves? Should governmental agencies assume that responsibility? Should private organizations? Should individuals? Third, how should we help? Should we give people food or teach them how to earn their own food? Fourth, once we start helping them, how do we move them from dependence to independence in the shortest possible period of time? Fifth, what is the effect of the assistance? Are we really helping them or preventing them from learning how to care for themselves? Are we really helping to alleviate poverty or merely increasing the number of those who feel that someone else should support them? Sixth, how much of our excess should we contribute to the poor? Seventh, how should we channel that assistance? Eighth, what type of assistance should we provide?"

"That sounds good, but I think you are just using that list to avoid helping the poor yourself."

"I do help the poor."

Not expecting such a reply after listening to his comments on poverty, the hostess commends him and invites an elaboration, "That is wonderful. I admire you and others like you so much. What do you do? Maybe I will get some ideas for what I can do."

"I pay taxes, up to fifty percent of my income including state and local taxes plus the hidden taxes on all the products we buy and the services we utilize."

With obvious disappointment in her voice Marge replies, "So do I, but what does paying taxes have to do with those in need? I am talking about what we can do to help the poor. They do not have enough, and we have more than we need."

"Paying taxes has more to do with it than most people realize. Think about it. The reality of life is that we all must consume some wealth to survive. We must eat, clothe ourselves, have some type of shelter, have medical care when become sick, etc."

"That's true for sure. I agree with that."

"Where does that wealth come from? We either have to have it, or we create it by working or investing, or some else provides it for us."

"That's understandable."

"Another reality of life is that some people either have or create more wealth than they need to survive while others either have or create less."

"That's what I was talking about. Some people have more than they need while others do not have enough."

"Exactly, and our political leaders have devised a tax system designed to help provide for the needs of the underprivileged. They take wealth from those who have or produce more wealth than they need to survive and redistribute it to those who do not have or produce enough for their needs. Thus, because of the redistribution system built into our tax system, a large percentage of our tax dollars is used by our government to care for us."

"Are you sure?"

"I'm not making it up. It's a fact."

"Where does the money come from?"

"From us. We pay the bills. Of the Internal Revenue tax collections we taxpayers pay 85.7%. Corporations pay 11.6%, which, of course, is passed on to consumers in the form of higher prices. Corporations do not pay taxes; only people pay taxes. Excise taxes account for the remaining 2.7%."

"Well, how much of that money goes to help people in need?"

"It's difficult to determine because prevailing government policy is to take care of all of us. Each of us is supported to some extent by various programs plus the existence of a safety net for those with the greatest need. In the 1996 Clinton budget Social Security and Medicare accounted for a third of the expenditures. In addition, there were numerous funds of welfare programs for the poor. Excluding national defense and interest payments on the national debt most of the funds in the 2000 budget were targeted for different government entitlement programs."

"I had never thought about that."

"Well, you should. You may want to give more and do more, but you should not feel guilty thinking that you are doing nothing. If you work and pay taxes, you certainly are making a contribution to the financial support of many citizens and other people living in America. There is no need to feel guilty. If you are working and/or investing to produce wealth, you are helping the economy and the poor."

The Globvs

Space ship SRP2112PRS glides swiftly through its assigned territory. Patrol Agent PA001100AP sits rigidly erect at the controls. Only his eyes move. Slowly, mechanically they sweep back and forth. Radar-like they search the outer fringes of the semi-darkness. His duty is to find and eliminate any space garbage that drifts into the atmosphere of Pater's Planet.

Spotting a faint reflection to his right, he reports to base control that he has sighted an intrusion. Permission to investigate is granted, and he swings his craft toward the unidentified object.

Within seconds the ship slips into a state of suspended motion inches from a small object. Out goes the mechanical retriever and in comes a capped metal cylinder.

"That's strange. We've never seen anything like this before," he puzzles. "This certainly looks nothing like the other floating junk that we've found."

A quick test reveals that the container and its contents are not dangerous. He is about to dispose of such a seemingly insignificant item when a normally dormant curiosity surfaces in his consciousness.

"We wonder if there is anything inside?" he thinks, testing the cap. At first, nothing; then the cap slowly turns as he applies increased pressure. Hesitatingly, he peeks inside. Paper. Sheets of paper rolled up to fit inside.

Like an errant child who knows he is being disobedient he pulls out the paper, sees that it has almost indecipherable writing on it, and responds to the plea at the top of the first page.

WHOEVER YOU ARE, PLEASE READ OUR STORY.

FOR YOUR OWN SAKES PLEASE READ IT.

We are beyond help. In the beginning it was not so; nor did we expect ever to fall, no to rush willingly and gleefully, into the inescapable trap that now surrounds us all. The power is too great. They have gained control.

I am hiding in my closet, and I have to write in the dark. Some way I must get the details of our downfall out to others.

The saddest part of our story is that we ourselves are to blame. We wanted the globvs, (The letter "o" is pronounced as is the "o" in the word "gob".) and we encouraged their growth. Yes, we did. We certainly did. At first, we eagerly planted and joyfully reaped the benefits, and later we made excuses, turned our head, and hesitated when our plantings began to grow beyond the limits we had anticipated. Strange, almost incomprehensible in retrospect, how we could have deceived ourselves so easily. How could we have let ourselves come to this? But I am getting ahead of myself. First the beginning, so you will understand what happened to us.

No one knows where the seeds came from, but I am sure that some of us planted them.

What did we plant? The globvs, of course.

What is a globv? A globv is the most wonderful, at first, and amazing plant that any of us had ever seen. Its leaves are bright and shiny, a translucent green that seems to have magical qualities. How they fascinated us. We could see all of our dreams coming true in those leaves, and no dream is so spellbinding as the one that promises all to all for nothing.

Our people quickly came to rely on these green leaves and to use them in ever increasing quantities. Brewed, they make a tranquilizing tea that is astonishingly addictive. Even those who find its taste bitter at first are rarely able to resist the urge to taste again and again until nothing else satisfies their thirst. Dried, they make a mild-tasting tobacco with profound effects. Smokers like the initial sensations and soon develop a euphoric feeling of bliss and security. Collected in mats, they make a very soft, comfortable bed. Sleep comes almost immediately as a faint, sweet aroma floats slowly upward gently lifting troublesome burdens from weary shoulders.

And the fruit. Luscious, red globvs about the size of a large apple hang abundantly within reach winter and summer, spring and fall, wet or dry. Strange that the weather doesn't seem to affect them at all. We should have suspected from the first that this was an unnatural plant, but being able to pick one's fill of fresh fruit year round was so delightful that no one could resist. Good, too. Delicious, in fact. Globvies, as we call them, seem to have a special taste that pleases everyone whatever the preference: dry or juicy, sweet or sour, crisp or mellow.

Globvs cast a special shade, also, which we had never envisioned. It cools in the summer and heats in the winter. Can you imagine? We did not really comprehend how such a tree could be, but questioning our good fortune was out of the question. Wow! What a super plant!

Word spread like a high wave washing over the sand at the beach, and our delighted people soaked up the news like thirsty sponges. We clamored for seeds, I'll tell you. At first, the demand just could not be met, but eventually we all had our seeds in the ground eagerly anticipating our very own globv. And how they grew. All they needed was to have someone put the seed in the ground. With only minimal fertilization, water, and cultivation they grew phenomenally well in all types of soil.

We did not have to wait long. Their growth was practically imperceptible, but it occurred nevertheless. Inches appeared unobtrusively day by day. One suddenly realized that new branches were where before there had been none. Within a year the first fruits were ready. Within another year there were enough globvies for everyone.

How happy we were. I can still remember the joy of that summer. We stopped tending our gardens. Why waste our time and energy when the globvies were better, and without the work, without the work. We swam, played tennis, canoed, hiked, or just sat around in our air-conditioned globv shade talking about how tough it used to be. The good life was no longer just around the corner. We had it, and we meant to take advantage of it. Even knowing what happened later, I must admit that those were the days. Strange about our people--we have always been optimists. We dream dreams even during our nightmares.

Well, I must not dwell on our total ecstasy and contentment during the first globv year. Such bliss was not to last, and I must hasten to warn you that the joy is ephemeral and deceptive.

Oh, we were not shocked into resolute counteraction by any sudden and noticeable changes. No, as stealthily and shrewdly as a serpent slipping slowly and silently toward its mesmerized victim we were engulfed in globv branches at the very time we were reveling in the benefits bestowed upon us. Even now I am not sure when I first became aware of what was happening. Many people still have not realized. Their globv keeps them comfortable and full--conditions that maximize a feeling of physical well being and minimize intellectual considerations of one's overall well being. No, they look no farther than their globv, and they're happy. They do not think about what is happening. They can not blame the globv. Of their own volition they place themselves under its control.

Maybe it was the day my satisfied mind stopped to focus on the fact that my expanding lower abdomen was obstructing passage of the zipper on my pants for the second year in as many seasons.

"Dear, how many times do I have to ask you to let the seat out in my pants?"

Her reply startled me. "I have, dear. The problem is not the size of the pants but the dimensions of what you are attempting to squeeze into them."

"How much did I weigh last year?"

"180."

"And the year before that?"

"160."

"Gee, that's forty pounds in two years. You've gained weight, too. When did we get the globv?"

"Two years ago."

"I thought so. Now that I think about it we're all getting fat. Lethargic, too. I wonder .?"

Or maybe it was the day my older daughter, Kathy, came stomping angrily into the house.

"What's the matter, dear?" my wife inquired.

"Oh, it's that awful globv," she retorted.

"Kathy, don't you even think such a thing! We couldn't get along without the globv."

"Well, you tell it to leave me alone. It won't let me sunbathe! Every time I move to a new spot it shades me."

At that point I began to ponder where we might be headed. I had not minded terribly when a globv sprang up, first one in the corner and then another in the front of the house near the driveway. They were all over. No one stopped to consider that self-propagation of something good might be bad in the long run. No, we all loved globvies, so we followed the simple logic--one globv good; two globvs better; three globvs even better, and on and on.

What should have been immediately obvious to everyone, but was not, soon began to happen. The natural plant life began to die. Nationwide an army of reluctant weekend trimmers and mowers shouted their wholehearted approval and sat back contentedly to have another globvie.

However, the days of leisure gradually disappeared. The ever growing globvs began to require more and more cultivation, more and more fertilizer. In no time their appetite for care matched our own for globvies. My family and I worked constantly catering to the globvs in order to maintain our globvies habit. Others, too, found themselves in the same situation. Unable, or unwilling, to curb their globvies appetite, they were forced to spend longer and longer periods of time satisfying the demands of their globvs.

The globv in the back near the patio slowly began to irritate my normally easy-going spouse.

"Dear, that globv makes me nervous."

"The globv? Are you kidding? How can a globv make you nervous?"

"It watches me all the time."

"Come on. A globv doesn't have eyes, and it can't watch you. Calm down."

However, I skeptically agreed to put that premise to the test. We started watching our globvs very carefully. Out of the corner of our eye, of course, because we did not want them to know that we were watching to see if they were watching. And slowly but surely we knew. They were. Gradually we became aware of their incredible capacities. There was no doubt of it. They were watching us all the time. They could sense what we were doing.

As soon as they realized that we knew of their vigilance, all dissimulation ceased. They openly followed our movements, and shortly the frightening potential and eventual goal of these demon globvs became evident. They intended to become our masters. The shade, the fruit, the ease of cultivation, at first, was only a cleverly-planned deception, an initial step in their plan.

We soon detected that globvs can smile and frown. They can wag their leaves in vigorous negatives or flutter mildly in gentle approval of our actions. Sometimes we received their approval, and sometimes their disapproval. Almost imperceptibly we acquired the unconscious habit of glancing in their direction to check their reaction. Behavior modification it is called in psychology classes, but they are such subtle masters of the art that their efforts are not terribly obnoxious. Besides, we were as hooked as anyone else on globvies in spite of our occasional nervous doubts, and we were unquestionably confident that we as thinking, rational individuals were masters of our fate and properly safe from globv domination.

I might never have awakened fully except for the day they went too far too fast. I had just gotten into my car and was starting to back out of the driveway, but the car would not move. The motor was racing, but the car remained motionless.

"What is going on?" I mutter to myself.

The mystery is partially explained as soon as I get out of the car. The globv near the driveway has locked the car in its branches and is frowning fiercely. I have done something wrong, but what? What? Is something wrong with the car? No, I just had it inspected.

Suddenly, it dawns on me. Of course! The seat belt. I had forgotten to fasten the seat belt. That must be it. I look up to see the globv smiling and nodding its approval.

Fury consumes me like a raging sea. "You have gone too far this time, you damn fiend," I shout, grabbing the ax and running toward the globv, looking for its main stem. Its leaves fly in my face. Its branches scratch my hands and tear at my clothes as I struggle to get closer, closer to the heart. Now I know. The globv must be trimmed and controlled, or we're lost.

Necessity of survival drives me on. Fiercely, desperately I push forward, hacking and cutting toward the hidden center.

Which is the one? Which is the one? Clearing the leaves out of my face and summoning all my strength I raise the ax for a fatal plunge into the center of the swirling, vibrating, impenetrable, incomprehensible mass in front of me. Screeching like a savage, I lunge forward bringing the ax downward with all my might.

"Take that, you monster!" I scream.

Suddenly, my wrists are almost broken as the ax is wrenched from my clinched fists at the height of its force. In an instant, I the attacker become the potential victim.

Stunned, I stare in amazement as tiny twigs slowly but surely start to coil around my waist. Fear freezes my arms and legs. My eyes bulge in terror as larger branches curl in slow motion around my chest. Onward, slowly onward they creep in their sinister mission. My legs start to grow numb. Breathing soon requires a special effort to overcome the contracting force of the branches. I feel as if I am in the middle of a terrible dream. "Get out! Get out before it's too late!," my subconscious signals in terror.

I struggle to free my arms and legs from the clutching branches. Only my survival instinct has been sufficient to stimulate my entrapped body to protect itself before it is slowly squeezed into oblivion.

"Jan! Jan! Help me! Quick!"

My wife opens the door to see what is the matter. Totally unprepared for the horrifying struggle before her, she instantly recoils. Her first instinctive reaction is that of self-preservation. She slams the door.

"Jan! Help me! Help me! Hurry!"

The door opens again. Emboldened by a primeval instinct, Jan rushes out to help me. Savagely she tears at the creeping coils as they move relentlessly to complete their fatal entrapment. Desperately, I join in the attack clawing at the writhing tentacles pulling me into the menacing mass. Somehow, energized by our terror and filled with an unsuspected strength, we succeed in twisting free from the branches twined around me.

Panting, bleeding and faint from fright, we stagger exhausted into the house, slam the door, and collapse on the floor. We are safe for the moment.

. . . .

Now I am a prisoner. I have not left the house for three months. The globvs are everywhere. Big ones, middle-sized ones, and little ones. We don't have to plant the seeds anymore, and the original globvs are growing and getting bigger with more and more branches. They are too big and complex. No one can find the center. And all the while they are sucking more and more energy and nutrients out of the land and the people.

Here I sit in a black cavern of hopelessness emasculated by the impenetrable mass surrounding us. Outside the globvs smile smugly, safe in the knowledge that the morass is too complex to unravel. The control must be there, but probably even the globvs do not know where. They are safe, and I am lost. Give up and give in. What other choice do I have? How can one fight what one can not comprehend? How can one combat and survive that which maintains that its sole function is to do good to you? How?

I can't write anymore. I hear a scratching at the window. It wants me. I know it does.

DON'T PLANT THE SEEDS! DON'T PLANT THE SEEDS!

. . . .

"Patrol Agent PA001100AP, you have now been stopped for ten minutes. Move on or explain your delay."

"Yes, Control. We are proceeding at once."

PA001100AP immediately deposits the container and its message in the incinerator and swooshes off into the black emptiness before him, all the while snickering incredulously, "What an absurd story. Why should we plant any seeds? Pater 1 gives us everything we need."